Active Imagination in Theory, Practice and Training

I0095035

Based on extensive research and developed with the support of the IAAP, this fascinating new work presents the precious value of the special legacy of C.G. Jung, which he himself defined as Active Imagination, through a collection of unpublished contributions by some of the brightest Jungian analysts and renowned representatives from the worlds of Art, Culture, Physics and Neurosciences.

In addition to presenting the genesis, development and results of Chiara Tozzi's research on Active Imagination, this volume on Theory, Practice and Training will also include the fundamental theoretical aspects of this technique. The book explores Active Imagination in relation to fundamental contents of Analytical Psychology, such as Individuation, Transformation and comparison with the Shadow, the four psychological functions, C.G. Jung's *Red Book*, and more. Moreover, the connections between Active Imagination and Sandplay will also be explored, as well as the possibilities of applying the technique with adolescent patients, how it's considered and proposed in Jungian Training, and some innovative clinical methodologies of Active Imagination.

Spanning two volumes, which are also accessible as standalone books, this essential collection will be of great interest to Jungian analysts, psychologists, psychoanalysts, or anyone interested in discovering more about the fascinating psychotherapeutic practice of Active Imagination and its interdisciplinary uses.

Chiara Tozzi is a Psychologist and Psychotherapist. She is a Training Analyst and Supervisor of *Associazione Italiana di Psicologia Analitica (AIPA)* and of the *International Association for Analytical Psychology (IAAP)*. She is also a Writer, Screenwriter, and Screenwriting Professor. She is Artistic Director of the '*Mercurius Prize*', based in Zurich.

Active Imagination in Theory, Practice and Training

The Special Legacy of C.G. Jung

Edited by Chiara Tozzi

Routledge
Taylor & Francis Group

LONDON AND NEW YORK

Designed cover image: Getty Images

First published 2024
by Routledge
4 Park Square, Milton Park, Abingdon, Oxon OX14 4RN

and by Routledge
605 Third Avenue, New York, NY 10158

Routledge is an imprint of the Taylor & Francis Group, an informa business

© 2024 selection and editorial matter, Chiara Tozzi; individual chapters, the contributors

British Library Cataloguing-in-Publication Data
A catalogue record for this book is available from the British Library

ISBN: 978-1-032-53301-8 (hbk)
ISBN: 978-1-032-53300-1 (pbk)
ISBN: 978-1-003-41136-9 (ebk)

DOI: 10.4324/9781003411369

Typeset in Times New Roman
by Apex CoVantage, LLC

To my masters,
to my patients,
to my students.

Contents

About the Editor

Chiara Tozzi is a Psychologist and Psychotherapist. She is a Training Analyst and Supervisor of *Associazione Italiana di Psicologia Analitica* (AIPA) and of the International Association for Analytical Psychology (IAAP). She is also a writer, screenwriter and screenwriting professor. She lectures internationally, and is a Visiting Professor to different IAAP Developing Groups. She is author of an International Research on Active Imagination supported by the IAAP, to be published by Routledge. She is Artistic Director of the international "Mercurius Prize for Films of Particular Psychological Significance and Sensitivity to Human Rights", based in Zurich. She is former editor of *Studi Junghiani*, the journal of the AIPA.

Contributors

Antonella Adorisio is a Training and Supervising Jungian Analyst with CIPA and IAAP. Past Director of Programming and Training at CIPA – Institute of Rome. Past Member of CIPA National Executive Board, she was President of the 17th CIPA National Congress in 2016. Antonella is a Registered Psychologist, Psychotherapist, Dance Movement Psychotherapist and Art Psychotherapist. She has been internationally teaching Active Imagination for many years. As a teacher of Authentic Movement, she studied with Janet Adler and Joan Chodorow. She leads international workshops on Authentic Movement and since 2004 she has been collaborating with Joan Chodorow as co-leader at the Pre-Congress day on Movement as a form of Active Imagination at the IAAP international congresses (Barcelona, Cape Town, Montreal, Copenhagen, Tokyo, Vienna). She is the author of numerous papers on Active Imagination, Authentic Movement, Body/ Psyche connections and the Feminine published in Italy, the UK and the USA. She has co-edited several books. She works and teaches mainly in Rome. She has been invited to lecture and teach in Kiew, Bucharest, Malta, Singapore, Zurich and in several Italian cities. She is still teaching Authentic Movement at ISAP Zurich as Guest Teacher. She is working with the IAAP Training Router Program in Romania. She filmed and edited the film-documentary "Mysterium – A Poetic Prayer-Testimonials on Body/Spirit Coniunctio", offered in many countries. The DVD was distributed by Spring Journal Books.

Gaetana Bonasera, PsyD, is a Jungian Analyst, IAAP and AIPA Member. She graduated in Psychology from Sapienza University of Rome. She obtained supervised systemic-relational psychotherapy training, a Master's in Hypnosis and Ericksonian Psychotherapy, and a master's in Emergency Psychology and Psychotraumatology. PsyD Bonasera has been working as a private psychotherapist for more than 20 years. Since 2018, she has been a Member of the DUN-Onlus Association that provides psychological support to migrants and refugees. She attended the AIPA Training Seminar on Active Imagination by Chiara Tozzi in 2019. She was also a speaker at the conference on Active Imagination by Chiara Tozzi: "Who Is Afraid of Active Imagination?" (AIPA, Rome 2019) as well as in the seminar by Chiara Tozzi "From Horror to Ethical Responsibility" (AIPA, Milan 2020).

"This remarkable and exciting book brings C.G. Jung's Active Imagination to the creative, scientific, spiritual, and transdisciplinary needs of the twenty-first century. Perspicaciously rooted in Jung, the book reinvents the clinical and provides essential steppingstones for those taking this practice into art, philosophy and the synchronistic sciences. With this collection, Chiara Tozzi establishes herself as an important voice in analytical psychology and its multiple capacities to energize knowing and being."

Susan Rowland

"This book offers a series of articles covering a wide scope with the aim of restoring Active Imagination to its rightful place as a significant method to access the unconscious and meaning in Jungian analysis. Active Imagination is a method developed by C.G. Jung which allowed him to access and delve into the images of his inner world and of the unconscious in order to more clearly understand their meaning and significance following the painful separation from Freud in 1913. The images and dialogues that emerged were recorded in the Red Book, which was kept private till its publication in 2019. The novelty of this method and the unusual images that emerged initially created concern in those around Jung and led some to question whether he was not falling into a state of psychosis. In fact, Jung was later very clear that it was precisely the use of Active Imagination and of the powerful images and dialogues that emerged as a result that enlightened him and led to a more profound understanding of the unconscious and of its archetypal contents. One of the legacies of the history of these early years is that there remains a lingering skepticism or mistrust with regard to the use and validity of Active Imagination. As a result, other than in training programs in Zurich, Active Imagination is often not given much attention. The editor of this book Chiara Tozzi sets out to address this lacuna and to restore Active Imagination to its rightful place as an invaluable avenue to access a living experience of psyche and of the unconscious in a personal manner. She manages this by bringing to the table, contributions from esteemed Jungian analysts who descrive their use of Active Imagination in clincial practice, which can include dialogues with dream figures, painting, meditation, body movement and dance. In addition, she has included voices from the world of the arts by inviting a director film/critic, a script writer, a professional dancer, a painter, an author, and a musician to reveal, from their unique and personal perspective, the central role that Active Imagination played in giving form to their creativity and of this method as a way of accessing the ephemeral from which meaning can emerge. The result is a wide-ranging collage of personal testimonies that attest to the usefulness of Active Imagination as a way to access the creative and the imaginal, in clinical practice, in ther arts and in our daily lives as an avenue to find meaning. This book will appeal not only to analysts, therpaists and artists but to everyone interested in their inner world and in creative expression. I highly recommend this book and am confident it will nourish many in their search for access to creativity and meaning in their lives."

Tom Kelly

"The strength of this book lies in its rich tapestry of voices. It is impressive to learn about the applicability of Active Imagination in scientific, artistic, and cultural fields. The editor has masterfully gathered together an exceptional collaboration of authors that offers a multifaceted exploration of Active Imagination, providing readers with a treasure trove of insights and perspectives. Across the two volumes of this book, theory, practice, and research are assembled in a very creative way that includes research, methodology, theory and practice. Readers will find references to personal experiences and practical examples that help us understand the transformative power of Active Imagination as an indispensable attitude and tool in all creative processes and encounters with the unconscious. Real-life applications and personal anecdotes add depth and authenticity to this book. I am sure that Chiara Tozzi's two-volume book on Active Imagination: *Active Imagination in Theory, Practice and Training: The Special Legacy of C.G. Jung (vol 1)* and *Interdisciplinary Understandings of Active Imagination: The Special Legacy of C.G. Jung (vol 2)* is a signigicant contribution that keeps the spark alive of one of C.G. Jung's most important legacies."

Pilar Amezaga

"Chiara Tozzi presents her research on the essential factor in analytical work that makes Jungians unique. Active Imagination is engagement with the psyche that speaks in images from within and from without. In this process one is guided by the wisdom of the Self that moves the development of the personality towards increased consciousness and wholeness. Tozzi clarifies that it is a process specific to the individual rather than a "technique". It furthers engagement with our fears and the unknown leading to the *Transcendent Function* that results in profound changes in our personality. Conversely though, it is this hard work and frightening engagement that deter many from its use. This book challenges us with a reminder of C.G. Jung's deeply effective creative path to healing."

Nancy Swift Furlotti

Laner Cassar is a Jungian Analyst (IAAP) from Malta. He is also a registered clinical Psychologist, Psychotherapist and Supervisor working with mental health services, and currently heads the Psychology Department at the Gozo General Hospital/Steward Health Care Malta. He hails from the "Essex school of analytical psychology" of the Centre for Psychoanalytic Studies, University of Essex, UK, where he earned his PhD in Psychoanalytic Studies. He is also an independent researcher in the history of psychoanalysis, analytical psychology and imaginative psychotherapy. Dr Cassar is engaged in various local and international educational institutions. He has written several publications on his main interest, namely the use and application of imagination in psychotherapy. His latest book was published by Routledge in 2020 and is entitled *Jung's Technique of Active Imagination and Desoille's Directed Waking Dream Method – Bridging the Divide*. He is the President of the Malta Depth Psychological Association, Director of SITE (Malta) and the International Network for the Study of Waking Dream Therapy (INSWDT).

Valerio Colangeli, IAAP and AIPA Analyst, is a clinical Psychologist and Psychotherapist. He collaborates with a social cooperative non-profit organisations as an operator in some residential and semi-residential psychiatric services of the ASL-RM1, with both adult and adolescent patients. He also has a private practice. He is the author of publications in Italian and in international journals. His main fields of research are analytical work in institutions and symbolic play in adolescence. He attended the AIPA Training Seminar on Active Imagination by Chiara Tozzi in 2019. He was also a speaker at the conference on Active Imagination by Chiara Tozzi: "Who Is Afraid of Active Imagination?" (AIPA, Rome 2019) as well as in the seminar by Chiara Tozzi "From Horror to Ethical Responsibility" (AIPA, Milan 2020).

Federico De Luca Comandini is a Jungian IAAP Analyst who graduated from the C. G. Jung Institute Zurich. He trained under D. Baumann and M. L. von Franz. He is a Member of the International Association for Analytical Psychology (IAAP), International Association of Graduate Analytical Psychologists, Zurich (AGAP) and Ordinary Member and Teacher at the Associazione Italiana Psicologia Analitica (AIPA). He holds seminars and participates as a speaker at conferences in Italy and worldwide. He carries out research on symbolism, in particular on the psychological processes involved in imagination. He is the author of many publications, including *L'Immaginazione Attiva. Teoria e pratica nella psicologia di C. G. Jung* (2002, curated with R. Mercurio), *In dialogo con l'inconscio* (2011) and *Quattro saggi sulla proiezione. Riverberi del Sé nella coscienza* (2013), with the contributions of R. Mercurio, D. Ribola and C. Widmann. He lives and practises in Rome.

Robert Mercurio is a Training Analyst and President of the Association for Research in Analytical Psychology (ARPA). After graduating in philosophy and then in management, he carried out his post-graduate studies in philosophy and theology at the Gregorian University in Rome. He then completed the training programme at the C.G. Jung Institute in Zurich where he got his diploma in Analytical Psychology.

Eva Pattis Zoja is a Jungian Analyst and Sandplay Therapist. She works in private practice in Milan, Italy. She is the founder of the International Association for Expressive Sandwork (IAES) and has offered training in Jungian Analysis and Sandplay Therapy in Europe, Asia, Latin America and Africa.

Murray Stein, PhD, is a Training and Supervising Analyst at the International School of Analytical Psychology Zurich (ISAP-ZURICH). He was President of the International Association for Analytical Psychology (IAAP) from 2001 to 2004 and President of ISAP-ZURICH from 2008 to 2012. He has lectured internationally and is the editor of *Jungian Psychoanalysis* and the author of *Jung's Treatment of Christianity, In MidLife, Jung's Map of the Soul, Minding the Self, Outside Inside and All Around, The Bible as Dream* and most recently *Men Under Construction*. He lives in Switzerland and has a private practice in Zurich.

Marta Tibaldi is a Psychologist, Psychotherapist, Jungian Analyst and Training and Supervising Analyst at IAAP and AIPA. From 2010 to 2019 she was the Liaison Person of the IAAP Developing Group in Hong Kong (HKIAP) and from 2012 to 2019 an applied Visiting Analyst in Taipei, Taiwan. She was an adjunct Professor of Intercultural Psychology at the University of Siena and a Consultant at the Italian Center of Solidarity "Don Mario Picchi Onlus" in Rome. Since 2008, she has been a teacher at the AIPA's analytical High School in Rome. Lecturer in national and international congresses and workshops, and author of many articles and essays, she has published the books *Il mito delle isole felici nelle relazioni di viaggio del Sette-Ottocento* (with G. Mazzoleni, D'Anna, Messina-Firenze 1975); *Oltre il cancro. Trasformare creativamente la malattia che temiamo di più* (Moretti & Vitali, Rome 2010); *Pratica dell'immaginazione attiva. Dialogare con l'inconscio e vivere meglio* (La Lepre, Rome 2011; enlarged edition published in Mandarin by PsyGarden Publishing, Taiwan and in simplified Chinese by Beijing ChenSheng Culture Communication Co. Ltd.); *Transcultural Identities. Jungians in Hong Kong* (with T. Chan, M. Chiu, M. Lee, B. Tam, E.T. Wong, Artemide Edizioni, Rome 2016); *Jung e la metafora viva dell'alchimia. Immagini della trasformazione psichica* (ed. with S. Massa Ope and A. Rossi; Moretti & Vitali, Bergamo 2020). She is the author of the blog "C.G. Jung's Analytical Psychology between Italy and China", now renamed "Conoscersi per conoscere". She also has a website and a video channel called "Marta Tibaldi. Psicologia analitica in un click".

Chapter 1

Active Imagination
The Special Legacy of C.G. Jung

Chiara Tozzi

The Pursuit of Active Imagination

The objective of this two-volume book on active imagination can be defined by two statements by C.G. Jung. I will begin with the first:

> The years when I was pursuing my inner images were the most important in my life – in them everything essential was decided. It all began then; the later details are only supplements and clarifications of the material that burst forth from the unconscious, and at first swamped me. It was the prima materia for a lifetime's work.
>
> (Jung, 1961, MDR, cap. VI p. 137)

When I read *Memories, Dreams, Reflections* for the first time in 1978, it was this very sentence, and the account of C.G. Jung's courageous confrontation with the unconscious, that particularly struck me. In the description of that dialogue and encounter with obscure and dangerous parts of oneself, which could fascinate but also instill horror, I found echoed the significant contents and images of the fairytales and legends that had captivated me as much as any other kid in childhood, regardless of the time and space in which that narration had taken place. And it was exactly from listening to and reading fairytales that a passion for storytelling was born in me, both as a mode of communication and as a profession, in literature and film.

When I started my training to become a Jungian analyst at Associazione Italiana di Psicologia Analitica (AIPA) in 1996, Dr Bianca Garufi, one of the most important Italian Jungian analysts, explained to me that this way of confronting the unconscious, first experimented by Jung on himself, was a real form of therapy, specific to Jungian clinical practice and referred to as active imagination.

Meeting Bianca Garufi resulted in a friendship that was precious to me. I met her at the making of the feature film *Le parole sono altrove*[1] (Tozzi *et al.*, 2000) with the AIPA Cinema Group. Bianca Garufi – with whom I had carried out one of the interviews needed to be admitted to the AIPA-IAAP Training – was the one who had invited me to join the AIPA Cinema Group because, although I was

DOI: 10.4324/9781003411369-1

then an AIPA trainee and not yet an AIPA-IAAP member, I had been a scriptwriter and screenplay teacher for over a decade. Bianca Garufi, in addition to being an AIPA-IAAP training analyst, was a recognized writer and poet: as a writer, she had published several books, including a novel written in four hands, including one of the most important Italian writers, Cesare Pavese (Garufi and Pavese, 1959). Here, I would like to recall one of her qualities as a poet – as I have done elsewhere: her splendid poem "Non l'Io" (Not the Ego; Garufi, 2002), referring precisely to the conversation between the Ego and the unconscious that takes place during the experience of active imagination. I was thus fortunate to have a first illustration of the complex and special essence of active imagination precisely through that "double-meaning" language that Bianca Garufi used spontaneously, and of which Jung speaks about his way of writing (von Franz, 1988): i.e. giving voice to a harmonious interaction between consciousness and the unconscious. Bianca Garufi, as an artist, could express herself and write in such a special way because she naturally possessed that more permeable diaphragm between consciousness and the unconscious (Jung, 1916/58), which for Jung is typical of creative people; yet, that more permeable diaphragm can be reached by anyone through the experience of active imagination, by virtue of the activation of the transcendent function, that is, that "movement out of the suspension between two opposites, a living birth that leads to a new level of being, a new situation" (Jung, 1916/58, par. 189).

The specificity of the therapeutic method Jung had identified and experimented on himself, i.e. active imagination, seemed to me extraordinary and valuable; at the same time, the fact that, during the six years of AIPA training and afterwards, I heard very little about it in the Jungian community was disconcerting.

Over time, I learned that this bizarre scotomization of a legacy that appears to be not only precious, but Jung's most specific clinical methodology compared with other psychoanalytical methods developed by famous scholars of the psyche, was not only taking place in Italy, but throughout the international Jungian community. Certainly, the publication of *The Red Book* (Jung, 2009) and its worldwide dissemination necessarily led to recognizing that "first matter for a lifetime's work" mentioned by Jung in *Memories, Dreams, Reflections*. But what else was that "first matter," so admirably depicted and described in *The Red Book*, if not precisely the contents of the unconscious that sprang from Jung's courageous experience of active imagination? And yet, while such contents and illustrations, after the publication of *The Red Book* by Sonu Shamdasani, became the object of in-depth study by the international Jungian community and anyone interested in the psyche, the same cannot be said for the dissemination of active imagination, which was also at the origin of those contents and illustrations. Focusing on one of the special qualities of *The Red Book*, namely its ability to symbolically illustrate a complex psychological journey through written and visual images that were never saturated, I decided to refer precisely to that double background used by Jung to explain his expository peculiarity. I therefore made a video, entitled *Un doppio fondo*,[2] in which I tried to summarize the affinities between the language of film and those of C.G. Jung's analytical psychology.

Encouraged by the feedback I received from some IAAP colleagues,[3] I continued to explore this connection between languages in light of active imagination, and followed up the screening of the video (the English version is called *En Route*) for the paper "En Route: From Active Imagination to Film Language," which I presented in 2013 at the 19th IAAP International Congress in Copenhagen (Tozzi, 2014).

After becoming a training analyst, in 2014 I was given the Seminar on active imagination at AIPA, which I have held every year since then (Colangeli, 2022). My first concern at the time was to try to pass on to AIPA trainees not only the theoretical aspect of active imagination, but what Jung had truly tried to pass on to us with his personal experience. In fact, I believe Jung does not *reductively and literally* tell us that what he wants to pass on and deliver is a pattern, a technique, or a method; rather, he leaves us a personal and suffered testimony, experienced first-hand, on *how* he symbolically lived the years when he practiced active imagination. His reluctance to present a "technical" pattern and outline of the practice of active imagination shows us how important it is to leave more space in the life of human beings for the individuative and transformative meaning and outcome of active imagination, as seen in *Memories, Dreams, Reflections* and in *The Red Book*.

Actually, I had and still have the impression there is a twofold approach within the Jungian community to the possibility of learning and teaching active imagination (Tozzi, 2023):

1 as a mainly mentalized repetition of a technique;
2 as a personalized integration of a different way of being in the world, of a capacity for equal confrontation with the unconscious, related to synchronicity and fundamental in the process of *individuation*.

The first and meaningful support to represent the approach I believed is most in line with the meaning given by Jung of active imagination (that is, the second one) came to me from Gerhard Adler's description of active imagination, in *Studies in Analytical Psychology* (Adler, 1948). In that essay, Gerhard Adler very efficiently clarifies the difference between the two approaches, arguing that one cannot speak of a

> "technique" of active imagination just as one can hardly speak of a "technique of dreaming" [. . .] By "active imagination" we understand a *definite attitude* towards the contents of the unconscious [. . .] The right attitude may perhaps be best described as one of "active passivity" [. . .] It is not unlike watching a film or listening to music [. . .] Only the difference is that in active imagination the "film" is being unrolled inside.
>
> (Adler, 1948, pp. 56–57)

To me, this brilliant and evocative explanation, based both on logic and on the metaphorical use of images, translated into a further image: that of "a different way of being in the world" (Tozzi, 2017), reachable through the individuative experience in active imagination. Based on this assumption, I decided to submit a proposal for the 20th IAAP International Congress to be held in Tokyo, Japan, in 2016. Before the Congress in Kyoto, a second contribution was fundamental to convince me that the journey I had embarked on in my research on active imagination truly made sense. As I have broadly described elsewhere (Tozzi, 2023, op. cit.), in the summer of 2015 I was at Yale University[4] to present "The Experience of Grace: The Possibility of Transformation in Vladimir Nabokov and Carl Gustav Jung" (Tozzi, 2015). There, I attended Murray Stein's incredible conference, "Synchronizing Time and Eternity: A Matter of Practice" (Stein, 2017). On that occasion, Stein's presentation was unfolding all my doubts and dilemmas related to my choice to teach, practice, and experience active imagination as an *attitude* and not as a *technique*. Actually, in his lecture, Stein presented an active imagination done by Pauli in 1953, stimulated by Jung and M.L. von Franz and defined by Pauli himself as "The Piano Lesson." In "The Piano Lesson," Pauli questioned himself on the same dilemma I was facing, represented in his active imagination, as follows: "There were two schools: in the older of the two one understood words but not meaning, while in the newer one understood meaning but not my words. I could not bring the two schools together" (Atmanspacher, Primus, and Wertenschlag-Birkhauser, 1995, pp. 317–330). Stein explained the two positions as follows:

At one level, this is a reference to the schools of nuclear physics and analytical psychology; at another level, it refers to the explanations that science offers and the meanings that derive from a depth psychological and spiritual orientation. Here Pauli was stuck.

(Stein, op. cit. p. 50)

As highlighted by Stein, to metaphorically represent this situation:

What he [Pauli, Ed.] came up with was a marvelous image, the piano, which with its black and white keys resonates with the Chinese yang-yin system. [. . .] But then it became a matter of learning "to play the piano," not only of understanding the issues intellectually [. . .]. This was the challenge put to him by Jung and von Franz.

(Stein, op. cit., p. 50)

After sharing Pauli's touching and meaningful active imagination, Stein added:

Pauli faces this issue head-on in this "active fantasy." The piano symbolizes a possible point of meeting. It represents the transcendent function, a synthetic mind. Of course, the question is: Can he play the piano? Well, he is learning. [. . .] At any rate, Pauli has given us in the image of the piano a useful metaphor for the transcendent function, which may assist our efforts to create a sustained and sustaining link between time and eternity for ourselves and with our patients.

(Stein, op. cit., pp. 55–56)

Following this inspiring lecture, when I was back in Rome I decided to write to Murray Stein, although I did not know him personally. I told him how much I had appreciated his lecture at Yale and I explained to him that, by presenting Pauli's active imagination on "The Piano Lesson," he had given a symbolic answer to my consideration on the two ways of experiencing and passing on active imagination. After all, my question on how to explain an attitude of active imagination had already been answered in the title of his lecture: it is . . . "A matter of practice"!

Ever since, all my detailed studies, conferences, and seminars on active imagination have been focused on trying to pass on to colleagues, patients, and trainees the meaning of that "different way of being in the world," given by a true experience of active imagination, as well as by the fascinating connections between active imagination and other forms of expression and of human research.

But . . . there is a but!

As I felt the enthusiasm and interest grow within me and received positive feedback on active imagination from many IAAP colleagues and trainees, both in Italy and in other countries I was visiting regularly as IAAP Visiting Professor, the dissemination and formation on this special Jungian method was still lacking.

When trainees asked me for a bibliography, I was forced to note there was a clear lack of publications in the field, especially compared with other topics that are more followed and analyzed within the Jungian community. I asked myself the reason for this scotomization, so unequal compared to such unique magnificence which we possess as Jung's followers. I came up with a possible answer: that, in fact, active imagination . . . scares. Nothing weird about that, considering the complex and delicate journey to undergo to reach a dialogue with the unconscious in a waking state, as required by active imagination. Yet, although understandable in patients and trainees, such blind fear is not comprehensible in Jungian analysts and, actually, seemed to me to be quite concerning. This is how I came up with the idea of addressing this "troublesome" issue at the 21st IAAP International Congress to be held in Vienna. I submitted my proposal of this difficult topic and I am thankful to my IAAP colleagues not only for accepting my presentation, but for inviting me to present "From Horror to Ethical Responsibility: Carl Gustav Jung and Stephen King Encounter the Dark Half Within Us, Between Us and in the World" in a plenary session. I must say that the unexpected and enthusiastic reaction by colleagues on that occasion was an additional stimulus that pushed me to go full throttle and even more in-depth: I ventured into a collective research on active imagination that I could have presented to IAAP colleagues. My video-interview, "The Lighting of Shadow Images – Interview with Giuseppe Tornatore,"[5] shot in the projection room of Tornatore's office in August 2019, in which Oscar-awarded director Giuseppe Tornatore confronts himself with Jungian active imagination for the first time, was another important step that pushed me to carry on with my project.

The final spark came from something else, but I will talk about that at the end of this chapter.

Support and Cooperation for My International Research on Active Imagination

This book is therefore the result of my research on active imagination, carried out with the support of the IAAP.

My proposal was submitted to the IAAP Academic Sub-Committee in 2021, and was soon after approved and granted a fund.[6]

In my research project, I asked for, and received, the collaboration of many IAAP colleague analysts from different countries who were particularly interested and who specialized in active imagination. I also asked for, and received, contributions from experts in the worlds of Neurosciences, Physics, Art, and Culture. The Research Unit RISORSA – Social Research, Organization and Risk in Health – of DiSSE – Department of Social and Economic Sciences – of the Sapienza University of Rome, Italy also provided their collaboration.

Additional support was also given by Shannon Marie Clay, freelance interpreter and translator who supported me in editing the book and translating some of the chapters. I am really thankful to Shannon, the backbone of this entire journey.

Following, the final list of participants:

IAAP Analysts

1 Tozzi, Chiara, AIPA-IAAP, Italy
2 Adorisio, Antonella, CIPA- IAAP, Italy
3 Bonasera, Gaetana, AIPA-IAAP, Italy
4 Cassar, Laner, Malta Jung Developing Group-IAAP, Malta
5 Colangeli, Valerio, AIPA-IAAP, Italy
6 De Luca Comandini, Federico, AIPA-IAAP, Italy
7 Deligiannis, Ana, SUAPA-IAAP, Argentina
8 Fleischer, Karin, SUAPA, IAAP, Argentina
9 Méndez, Margarita, SVAJ-IAAP, Venezuela
10 Mercurio, Robert, ARPA, Italy[7]
11 Nieddu, Gianfranca, AIPA-IAAP, Italy
12 Pattis Zoja, Eva, CIPA, Italy
13 Renn, Regina, DGAP- IAAP, Germany[8]
14 Stein, Murray, AGAP-IAAP, Switzerland
15 Tibaldi, Marta, AIPA-IAAP, Italy

Representatives from the Worlds of Art, Culture, Neurosciences, and Physics, and Sapienza University of Rome, Italy

16 Aiolli, Giacomo, musician, Italy
17 Clay, Shannon Marie, linguist, Italy

18 Cogliati Dezza, Irene, research fellow in the Affective Brain Lab at University College London and Massachusetts Institute of Technology
19 Contarello, Umberto, scriptwriter, Italy
20 Padroni, Luca, painter, Italy
21 Piperno, Elsa, dancer, choreographer and dance teacher, Italy
22 Puddu, Emiliano, physics professor, Italy
23 Sesti, Mario, critic-journalist, Film Festival Director and Documentary Director, Italy
24 Voltolini, Dario, writer, Italy
25 Research Unit RISORSA – Social Research, Organization and Risk in Health – of DiSSE – Department of Social and Economic Sciences – of the Sapienza University of Rome, Italy[9]

Research Characteristics and Methodology

First Phase

My research on active imagination was a "qualitative" research which therefore required the necessary tools to translate qualitative data into quantitative data for the needed analysis and comparisons.

To this end, two "structured" questionnaires with predefined answers were provided for a numerical translation. One questionnaire was sent to IAAP members, trainees, and routers to verify their knowledge, appreciation, and clinical practice of active imagination. A second questionnaire was sent to the people in charge of IAAP training (IAAP training analysts) and covered the relevance given to active imagination during IAAP trainings.

The questionnaires were submitted through an online platform and, based on the answers received, were processed in progress by the Research Unit RISORSA of Sapienza University of Rome, Italy.

A report on the answers collected was sent to me, and I then forwarded the results to my IAAP colleagues who contributed to this research.

The results of the first phase were aimed at providing useful material for a personal processing and/or a collective discussion among IAAP analysts taking part in this research. The material was made available for analysts to use in their personal contributions to the research.

Second Phase

During the second phase, the IAAP analysts working on this research were free to choose whether they wanted to work by themselves on a topic related to active imagination, or to exchange opinions with myself and/or the other participants.

At the same time, during the second phase, additional contributions were provided by a neuroscientist and a physics professor, as well as contributions and amplifications from the world of contemporary culture and art.

The results of the questionnaires and the contributions and knowledge provided by participants could be shared collectively after I sent them out. This was aimed at favoring a network of connection and exchange among IAAP analysts taking part in the research, and among the neuroscientist and physics professor and all representatives from the world of culture and arts who decided to take part in this specific research development. This exchange could lead to further contributions aimed at providing detailed empirical studies as well as new and original content to corroborate the importance given by C.G. Jung to active imagination. Moreover, it could help to highlight that active imagination is a unique psychotherapeutic method, different from all the other methods available and practiced in psychoanalysis and psychotherapy.

The results of the research were collected in a structured database. From the beginning, a possible outcome of such data and all material produced and collected was to give life to a publication managed by me, as editor of this research.

The quality of the questionnaire was monitored by the Research Unit RISORSA of Sapienza University of Rome. I then analyzed the results of the questionnaire and summarized and interpreted them.

Trend of the Research

The research project started in 2021, stemming from the hypothesis that the theory and practice of active imagination, although fundamental and crucial in C.G. Jung's analytical psychology, are not well known, studied, and practiced within the Jungian community, and are very little known to all those who are not part of the purely psychoanalytical setting.

The first goal of my research was to:

1   Verify the truthfulness of the hypothesis through one questionnaire divided in two parts, as previously described. I designed and then prepared and managed the questionnaire with the support of the Research Unit RISORSA, DiSSE, Department of Social and Economic Sciences of Sapienza University of Rome, Italy.

The questionnaire was to be sent to all IAAP members, routers, and trainees, and IAAP training analysts.

Questionnaire Emerging Questions

   i How aware are IAAP members of active imagination?
  ii Was active imagination considered meaningful and valuable in C.G. Jung's clinical practice?
 iii How much importance is given by IAAP members to active imagination as a psychotherapeutic method?
 iv Which scientific, artistic, and expressive fields can be linked to active imagination?

   v To what level is active imagination used in Jungian psychotherapy?
   vi How much research is there on active imagination?
   vii Is active imagination properly addressed in IAAP training?
   viii How to bridge the possible gap at the level of training, knowledge, and clinical practice?

2 Analyze and evaluate the results of the questionnaires.
3 Prepare a database based on the scientific evidence of the theoretical knowledge, practice, and training of active imagination by IAAP analysts to support IAAP dissemination programs about active imagination at the international level.

Administration, Timing of Data Processing, and Validity of the Questionnaire

The questionnaire was carried out and processed by the Research Unit RISORSA – Social Research, Organization and Risk in Health – of DiSSE – Department of Social and Economic Sciences – of the Sapienza University of Rome, Italy

The survey was carried out from August 27 to October 15, 2021.

The questionnaires were sent by the IAAP Secretariat to 3,564 individuals among IAAP training analysts and IAAP members, and to 378 individuals among IAAP routers and trainees, for a total of 3,942 individuals.

Overall, 12.63 percent of the reference population answered the questionnaires.

The level of response was sufficient for an online survey and it could therefore be considered valid.

Interpretation of the Final Data of the Questionnaire

First consideration: although the questionnaire is valid, I think it is interesting to think about this: why didn't 87.37 percent – almost 90 percent! – of IAAP members respond to the questionnaire?

Only in a few countries was there a high response rate to the questionnaire. Among these, for IAAP members, routers, and trainees the highest response was recorded in:

United States	87
China	27
Italy	27
United Kingdom	24

For IAAP training analysts, the highest response was recorded in:

Germany	38
United States	27
Switzerland	17

Total Respondents by Country

COUNTRY	N	COUNTRY	N
Argentina	4	Italy	27
Australia	2	Japan	3
Austria	4	Latvia and Lithuania	1
Belarus	2	Lithuania	1
Belgium	3	Luxembourg	1
Brazil	23	Malta	3
Bulgaria	3	Mexico	2
Canada	12	Netherland	1
Chile	2	Peru	1
China	27	Poland	2
Colombia	1	Portugal	1
Czech republic	1	Romania	5
Denmark	5	Russia	11
Dominican Republic	2	Serbia	3
Estonia	1	South Africa	5
France	8	South Korea	3
Georgia	11	Spain	4
Germany	9	Switzerland	18
Hong Kong	1	UK	24
Hungary	1	Ukraine	6
India	5	Uruguay	2
International	1	USA	87
Ireland	1	Venezuela	2
Israel	2	**Total overall**	**344**

Figure 1 Table of IAAP member, router, and trainee respondents by country.

Total Respondents by Country

COUNTRY	N
Argentina	2
Australia	2
Austria	4
Brazil	8
Canada	5
Chile	1
China	3
Czech republic and the Netherlands	1
Denmark	3
Deutschland, schweiz	1
France	4
Germany	38
Israel	10
Italy	13
Italy and Switzerland	1
Japan	1
Russia	3
Serbia	1
South Africa	1
South Korea	1
Spain	2
Switzerland	17
UK	4
Uruguay	1
USA	27
Total overall	**154**

Figure 2 Table of IAAP training analyst respondents by country.

The first interesting result is seen in Germany, where only nine IAAP members, routers, and trainees answered the questionnaire (resulting among the lowest countries per response rate), while there was a high response rate among IAAP training analysts, accounting for 38 respondents and therefore positioning itself at the top of the list. This is an inverted trend compared with the rest of the countries, where there was a lower response rate among IAAP training analysts than among IAAP members, routers, and trainees. It is true that there are fewer IAAP training analysts than IAAP members, routers, and trainees in the different IAAP Associations, but it would be interesting to assess the results of the high or low number of training analysts who participated in the questionnaire. For example, in Italy, among all AIPA, CIPA, and ARPA training analysts – that is, 305 individuals – only 13 answered the questionnaire, accounting for 4.2 percent of all Italian IAAP training analysts. It may be useful and interesting for IAAP Associations in the different countries to calculate *ex-post* the percentage of training analysts who answered the questionnaire in each country.

Considering the results presented above, it appears that although IAAP members, routers, and trainees, and IAAP training analysts consider active imagination to be a meaningful component for C.G. Jung (95.3 percent and 90 percent, respectively) both at theoretical and clinical level, they are not adequately informed about such practice.

Among those who answered the questionnaire, only 48.7 percent of IAAP training analysts experienced active imagination as patients, 69 percent experienced it in training, and yet 81.9 percent use it in their clinical practice, showing that a large number of IAAP training analysts use active imagination even though they may not have personally experienced it during their analysis. This leads to a first interesting question: since many IAAP training analysts use the practice of active imagination without having experienced it as patients or trainees, are we truly able to provide the skills necessary to use active imagination in our clinical practice? Are we sufficiently trained to pass on the knowledge and practice of active imagination to IAAP trainees?

QUESTION: In your opinion, did C. G. Jung consider Active Imagination to be meaningful and valuable in his clinical practice?

Overall:

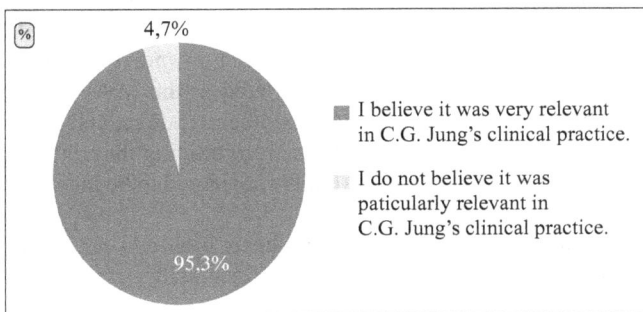

Figure 3 Percentage of IAAP member, router, and trainee respondents who believe and who do not believe C.G. Jung considered active imagination to be meaningful and valuable in his clinical practice.

QUESTION: *In your opinion, did C. G. Jung consider Active Imagination to be meaningful and valuable in his clinical practice?*

Overall:

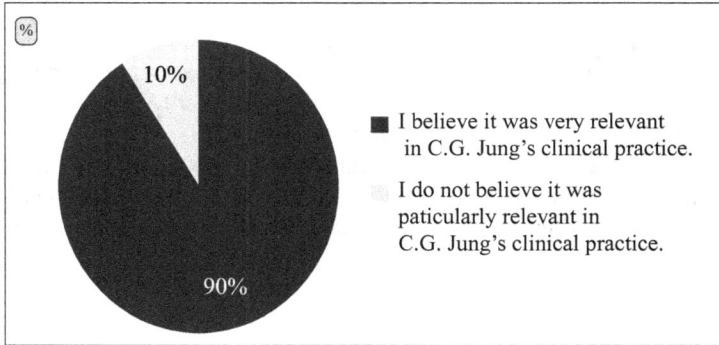

Figure 4 Percentage of IAAP training analyst respondents who believe and who do not believe C.G. Jung considered active imagination to be meaningful and valuable in his clinical practice.

Only 38.1 percent and 36.3 percent of all members, routers, and trainees are familiar with the scientific literature on active imagination in international journals and in their country's accredited journals of analytical psychology. For IAAP training analysts, the percentages account for 54 percent and 50.6 percent, leading us to think there may be a lack of stimuli on the subject. This seems to once again confirm that the knowledge on active imagination is not sufficiently widespread among members, routers, and trainees, nor among training analysts.

Moreover, 55 percent of IAAP training analysts say active imagination is considered to be an optional component in training.

Of the respondents, 56 percent believe it is seen as a secondary method; however, in reality, 78.8 percent of IAAP members, routers, and trainees consider it a fundamental component in training.

The percentage asking for more practical exercises on such content through experiential workshops is 83.7 percent. In addition, 42.2 percent of IAAP members, routers, and trainees consider active imagination to be a fundamental component in training, showing a further discrepancy between how individuals perceive active imagination and how they believe it is considered in the IAAP Association they are part of. Actually, 78.8 percent of IAAP members, routers, and trainees say that active imagination is a fundamental component in training, but only 33 percent of training analysts believe active imagination is considered to be an essential method in the Association they are part of.

Data analysis validates the research hypothesis highlighting, among others, a big discrepancy in the confidence shared by Jungian analysts who consider active

QUESTION: *Is Active Imagination considered to be*
an optional component in training?

Overall:

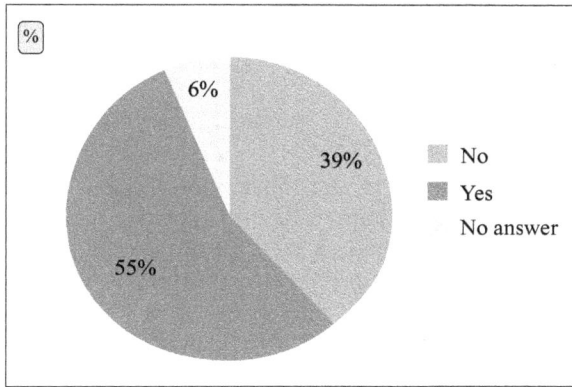

Figure 5 Percentage of IAAP training analyst respondents who believe and who do not believe active imagination is considered to be an optional component in training.

QUESTION: *Do you consider Active Imagination*
a fundamental component in IAAP training?

Overall:

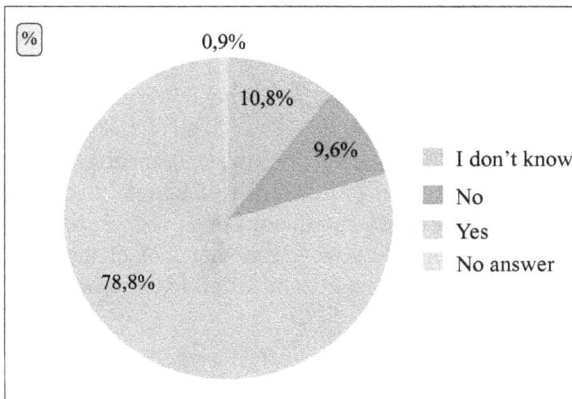

Figure 6 Percentage of IAAP member, router, and trainee respondents who believe, who do not believe, and who do not know if active imagination is considered to be a fundamental component in training.

imagination to be a fundamental practice both for C.G. Jung and for the Jungian community, and the current lack of knowledge, spread, use, and relevance of such practice by IAAP Jungian analysts and in IAAP training.

I believe all this material could represent some interesting food for thought on the relevance given to active imagination within the IAAP, both as theoretical knowledge and as clinical practice, and as a teaching subject in IAAP training.

Content and Aim of the Book

The aim of this book is to broaden and enhance the precious value of the special legacy of C.G. Jung, which he himself defined as active imagination, through a collection of unpublished contributions by some of the brightest Jungian analysts and renowned representatives from the disciplines of Art, Culture, Physics, and Neurosciences from different parts of the world.

About one century after the creation of C.G. Jung's active imagination, these voices put together give life to a multifaceted representation of active imagination, showing its many characteristics at a theoretical level, the different settings and ways in which such practice is currently used and experienced, and the resonance that active imagination can have in the scientific, artistic, and cultural fields.

The book not only targets the Jungian community, psychologists, and psychoanalysts in general, but also anyone in the world who may be interested in discovering the possible correlation between an original and fascinating psychotherapeutic practice such as active imagination, and the content in the fields of Neuroscience, Physics, Cinema, Literature, Painting, Music, and Dance.

I invited both fellow Jungian analysts and friends from the worlds of Art, Culture, Physics, and Neurosciences to work on this book, with the goal of offering the reader a kaleidoscopic representation of the extent to which active imagination, as conceived and experienced by C.G. Jung, is present. I allowed all authors complete freedom, and at the same time made myself available to collaborate, clarify, amplify, and listen. In fact, I can say I supported the writing of the chapters for at least half of the participants, helping them step by step. For me, this was a true way of diving into varied and differentiated fields and contents, always fascinating and interconnected.

The division into two volumes is intended to facilitate the reader's orientation in different subjects, but the areas and themes dealt with in both volumes are absolutely related to one another. Indeed, I hope that each chapter pushes readers to look for the possible amplification and completion in the others.

Active Imagination in Theory, Practice and Training. The Special Legacy of C.G. Jung

This volume mainly addresses the history, theory, clinical practice, and personal experimentation, as well as reflections on the teaching of active imagination. By simultaneously addressing the theoretical aspects and the practical application of active imagination through the method of "authentic movement", the last chapter is a sort of *trait d'union* between the first and the second volume.

Interdisciplinary Understandings of Active Imagination. The Special Legacy of C.G. Jung

In this volume, I deliberately wanted to give space to the close correlation between active imagination and the soma: the body, emotions, sensations, and feeling come into play, in the experience of active imagination, no less than what Jung defined as the "thinking function". Particular space is devoted, in this regard, to illustrating the practice of active imagination in the form of "authentic movement". This volume is also made up of the contributions and amplifications provided by the representatives from the worlds of Physics, Neurosciences, Cinema, Literature, Painting, Dance, and Music. This proves that all these areas can in some way have to do with active imagination.

Ways Participants Contributed to This Book

While, as already mentioned, fellow Jungian analysts had complete freedom of choice on the content to be developed, I asked the representatives of Art, Culture, Physics, and Neuroscience to compare their work with the four phases of active imagination, as described by M.L. von Franz (1980) as follows:

Phase 1: The first phase of active imagination can be defined as letting things happen. A deliberate emptying of one's mind, which Jung defined as doing-by-not-doing, a receptive abandonment, an inclination to opening up to images characterized by unselfconsciousness, and devoid of conscious controls, corrections, and denials.

Phase 2: The second phase of active imagination occurs when you can also accept the irrational and incomprehensible, because they both represent the process of becoming. An acceptance capable of allowing the unconscious images to surface to the consciousness.

Phase 3: The third phase of active imagination is that of recording of images transforming themselves. The progressive change of the contents of imagination is carefully followed and described, either by writing down the images or expressing them through other means, such as painting, sculpture, music, dance, etc.

Phase 4: In the fourth phase, when active imagination comes to life, an actual dialogue with the unconscious takes place, through an "ethical confrontation" with anything that was previously created. It is the individual stance, fundamental to really come to terms with one's inner images and Shadow. Jung turns the metaphor of theater around, speaking of "making the scene".

Last but not least, as rightly pointed out by Joan Chodorow, "later on" to these four phases, "she (von Franz, Ed.) adds: Apply it to ordinary life" (Chodorow, 1997, p. 11). This recommendation once again shows that active imagination cannot be compared to a technique since it suggests making active imagination natural and connatural to our way of being in the world. And this is directly related to what

I highlighted with regards to an attitude of active imagination and the consequent different way of being in the world.

I am extremely grateful to all analyst colleagues from the Jungian community for the stimulating contributions and analysis on active imagination provided to my research. I am also grateful to all my friends who are representatives of the worlds of Art, Culture, Physics, and Neurosciences for accepting the invitation to a confrontation with active imagination in relation to their professional field. It was extremely fascinating for me to receive their resonance, as a result of "only" perceiving the four phases of active imagination.

After two years of work, and thanks to the special legacy of active imagination passed on to us by C.G. Jung, interviewing and carrying out this research with the participants, through an ongoing dialogue and shared path, resulted in the creation of a very meaningful and fascinating interdisciplinary bridge.

I trust this fascination will reach all readers.

The Spark of Ethical Confrontation

As I said at the beginning of this chapter, this book on active imagination can be defined by two statements by C.G. Jung. The first, as previously described, is related to my initial and distant encounter, in 1978, with "the prime matter" at the core of Jung's work, namely active imagination. The second, on the other hand, had an affectively special function for me in the genesis of the research behind this book.

Between 2020 and 2021, during the difficult period of the COVID-19 pandemic, I decided to write a novel (Tozzi, 2022) on this: the search for something meaningful that has been lost, and which is essential to find again. Just as I was finishing reviewing the manuscript and reflecting on the title I had chosen, i.e. *La scintilla necessaria* (The Necessary Spark), I found myself rereading the last volume of Jung's *Letters III* (Jung, 1997), written between 1956 and 1961. And a sentence from one of them particularly struck me. The letter is dated 22 December 1958, and is addressed to Baroness Vera von der Heydt. Jung speaks precisely of active imagination, and how its application has been misinterpreted. Finally, he concludes: "From such discussion we see what awaits me once I have become posthumous. Then everything that was once fire and wind will be bottled in spirit and reduced to dead nostrums. Thus are the gods interred in gold and marble and ordinary mortals like me in paper" (Jung, 1975: 469).

As usual, the images Jung delivers are extremely powerful. And the image of Jung prefiguring himself buried only in paper resonates painfully. Even in later letters in 1960, Jung appears concerned about the fate of what he was attempting to convey which was not understood or was misunderstood.

Here, that reading, at such a collectively heavy and dark time, seemed to me an event related to synchronicity. I had just finished writing a story where it seems fundamental to keep "the necessary spark" alive: but what was I doing about the precious legacy handed down to us by Jung, to keep his spark alive? Such a question seemed to have a lot to do with that "ethical confrontation" which, for Jung, is the final goal of active imagination.

This is why that very evening I decided that, although the undertaking seemed disproportionate, I should try to start a research into active imagination.

First of all, I wrote to Murray Stein. Then, one by one, to other colleagues and friends.

And they all picked up that spark with me.

Notes

1 *Le parole sono altrove*, by Gruppo Cinema A.I.P.A, presented at the Congresso Nazionale A.I.P.A (Napoli 2000), and 15th IAAP International Congress, Cambridge, UK, August 2001.
2 *Un doppio fondo* [A double meaning] [Video], by Chiara Tozzi, Congresso Internazionale AIPA-IAAP "Jung 50 anni dopo", Roma, 2011.
3 Special thanks go to my colleague Tom Kelly. I don't think I would have had the courage to continue working on that research at the international level without his enthusiastic feedback after the viewing of *Doppio fondo* in Rome.
4 As part of the Fourth Joint Conference IAAP and IAJS: "Psyche, Spirit and Science: Negotiating Contemporary Social And Cultural Concerns", Yale University, New Haven, CT, July 2015.
5 *The Lighting of Shadow Images – Interview with Giuseppe Tornatore by Chiara Tozzi* was screened for the first time at the IAAP International Film and Analytical Psychology Conference, Belgrade, 2–4 June 2023.
6 I am extremely grateful to the IAAP officers back then: IAAP: Toshio Kawai (President), Misser Berg (President Elect), Pilar Amezaga (Vice President), Emilija Kihel (Vice President), Yasuhiro Tanaka (Honorary Secretary), as well as Pilar Amezaga and Grazina Gudaite, Co-Chair of the IAAP Academic Sub-Committee, for encouraging and supporting me in a task that, at the time, seemed just as big as it was risky. I am also grateful to the IAAP Secretary Selma Gubser for the patient and kind support provided with regards to sending and receiving back the questionnaire from all IAAP members.
7 Robert Mercurio translated the chapter by IAAP colleague Federico de Luca Comandini from Italian into English.
8 Regina Renn worked with me in developing the research. Although she decided from the start not to provide a written contribution, I am grateful for her ongoing support, advice, and encouragement.
9 Giorgio Banchieri, ASIQUAS National Secretary, DiSSE, Department of Social and Economic Sciences, teacher, Sapienza University of Rome and *Sapienza* e LUISS Business School, Rome; Paolo Fornelli, Researcher at DiSSE, Department of Social and Economic Sciences, Sapienza University of Rome, ASIQUAS member; Maria Piane, Researcher at the Faculty of Medicine, *Sant'Andrea*, Sapienza University of Rome, ASIQUAS member.

References

Adler, G. (1948) *Studies in Analytical Psychology*, London and New York: Routledge, 1999.
Atmanspacher, H., Primus, H., and Wertenschlag-Birkhauser, E. (eds.). (1995) *Der Jung-Pauli Dialog und seine Bedeutung fur diemoderne Wissenschaft* [The Jung–Pauli Dialogue and Its Significance for Modern Science], Berlin: Springer.
Chodorow, J. (ed.) (1997) *Jung on Active Imagination*, New York: Routledge.
Colangeli, V. (2022) "Active imagination": Interview with Dr. Chiara Tozzi", AIPA. https:// www.youtube.com/watch?v=9WSrMg_wVuI
Garufi, B. (2002) "La Poesia" [Poetry], in *L'Immaginazione Attiva, a cura di De Luca Comandini e Robert Mercurio* [*The Active Imagination* edited by De Luca Comandini and Robert Mercurio]. Milan: La Biblioteca di Vivarium.

Garufi, B., and Pavese, C. (1959) *Fuoco grande*, Turin: Einaudi. [Pavese, C. (1963), *The Beach: And, A Great Fire*, in Collaboration with Bianca Garufi., London: P. Owen Publisher.]

Jung, C.G. (1916/58) "The Transcendent Function", *Collected Works*, Vol. 8, Princeton: Princeton University Press, 1975.

Jung, C.G. (1961) *C.G. Jung, Memories, Dreams, Reflections*, London: Fontana Press 1995.

Jung, C.G. (1975) "Letters, Volume 2: 1951–1961", G. Adler & A. Jaffè (eds), Princeton: Princeton University Press.

Jung, C.G (1996) *Lettere, III*, Magi Edizioni, Rome 2006, p. 185 (C.G. Jung, *Briefe*, Patmos VerlagGmbHo, KG, Walter-Verlag, Dusseldorf, 1997).

Jung, C.G. (2009) *The Red Book: Liber Novus*, New York: Norton.

Stein, M. (2017) "Synchronizing Time and Eternity: A Matter of Practice" in *Outside, Inside and All Around*, Asheville, North Carolina: Chiron Publications.

Tozzi, C. (2014) "En Route: From Active imagination to Film Language" in *Proceedings of the 19th Congress of the International Association for Analytical Psychology*, Daimon Verlag.

Tozzi, C. (2015) "Jung &Nabokov", in Succedeoggi.it https://www.succedeoggi.it/2015/12/jung-nabokov/.

Tozzi, C. (2017) "A Different Way of Being in the World: The Attitude of the Patient Scriptwriter", *Journal of Analytical Psychology* 62(2), April 2017.

Tozzi, C. (2017) "A Different Way of Being in the World" in *Proceedings of the 20th Congress of the International Association for Analytical Psychology*, Daimon Verlag.

Tozzi, C. (2022) *La scintilla necessaria* [The Necessary Spark]. Mondadori, Milan.

Tozzi, C. (2023) "Active Imagination and Testament: A Window on the Other Side of Life", in *Individuation Psychology: Essays in Honor of Murray Stein*, Chiron.

Tozzi, C., *et al.* (2000) *Le parole sono altrove* [Words are elsewhere]. Film by Gruppo Cinema AIPA, Congresso Nazionale AIPA, Naples.

Tozzi, C., *et al.* (2001) *Le parole sono altrove* [Words are elsewhere]. Film produced by Gruppo Cinema AIPA, 15th IAAP International Congress IAAP, Cambridge, UK.

Von Franz, M.L. (1980) "On Active Imagination", in *Inward Journey: Art as Therapy*, 17 (La Salle and London: Open Court, 1983).

Von Franz, M.L. (1988) *Il mondo dei sogni*, Tea Due, p. 102, Milan, 1996 [*The Way of Dream*, by Fraser Boa, Windrose Films Ltd, Toronto, 1988].

Chapter 2

Active Imagination, Agent of Transformation in the Individuation Process

Murray Stein

The vital role of active imagination for individuation was established by Jung himself, and its centrality was rooted in his personal experience. This was described in chapter 6 of *Memories, Dreams, Reflections* (1961), titled "Confrontation with the Unconscious". The title of this chapter indicates the type of relationship between conscious and unconscious that Jung has in mind: it is a "confrontation". This word is a translation of the German *Auseinandersetzung*, which has a specific meaning that in English might be better translated as "dialogue", meaning by this an active discussion between two conversation partners that exposes similarities and differences between their respective views but does not lead to supremacy of one over the other or to repression of either side. The part that active imagination plays in psychological development is to offer an avenue for crossing the divide between ego-consciousness and ego-identity on the one side and the instinctual and archetypal forces of the unconscious on the other. The full story of how Jung used active imagination in his dialogue with the unconscious is told in *The Red Book: Liber Novus*, which was published only in 2009, nearly a century after its creation. In Jung's subsequent clinical practice, active imagination took a central role because of its effectiveness as an agent of transformation in the service of psychological development, i.e., individuation. Combined with working with dreams in analysis, active imagination proved to be crucial for achieving the maximum impetus toward facilitating the client's individuation.

Active imagination is a form of self-engagement, and it calls for the intentional introversion of psychic energy. Whereas extraversion directs a person's attention to the world around, introversion looks to the inner world which is made up of thoughts, feelings, images, intuitions, etc. Typically, most of an adult person's day is spent in the extraverted mode attending to business in the world around. Sometime, of course, this shifts. If you go to a concert, for example, you will most likely begin in the extraverted mode, observing people around you in the lobby, finding your seat, looking at the ceiling and stage curtain and so forth. When you listen to the music carefully and with full attention, what you are aware of is actually the vibrations in the air that are coming into your ears and being translated into brain waves. Your attention is taken up by the sounds that are coming to you from the orchestra. Sometimes, however, when you're listening

DOI: 10.4324/9781003411369-2

to music, you might start seeing images in your mind's eye, in your inner world, or you might see colors (synethesia) or some kinds of movement. Or you might start experiencing fantasy images—a landscape, a thunderstorm, people on the move or making love. If you start paying attention to what is going on in your imagination, you've changed modes from extraversion to introversion. Extraversion is listening to the sounds; introversion is observing how the sounds affect you emotionally or mentally. In your inner world, you engage with emotion, images, and thoughts.

Dreaming is pure introversion. In dreams, one is experiencing the inner world exclusively. This is obviously a realm of pure representation since our senses are not providing information from the outer world. Some philosophies argue that, in fact, we only experience the inner world, and what we take to be the outer world is a mental construction pure and simple. In psychology, however, there is a strong conviction that our senses and mental functions do give us an impression, perhaps not altogether accurate, of an external world. We make a distinction between inner world and outer worlds, although it is recognized that the two are entangled and often very difficult to separate because of the dynamics of introjection and projection.

Active imagination is a deliberate turning inward in an attempt to engage the background of the psyche's subjectivity as deeply as possible while in a waking state. It is a kind of meditation. We can draw contrasts and comparisons between dreaming and active imagination. Active imagination is similar to dreaming, only it is carried out whilst the subject is awake and therefore in control of the activity. Dreaming is the brain thinking, but in images and stories rather than in logical or rational sequences. Active imagination involves a similar type of thinking, also using images and stories rather than directed thinking. In dreams, we speak of a dream-ego, which participates actively or passively in the narrative. In active imagination, the subject-ego may also be active or passive, but it is so by choice. The subject chooses to be actively engaged in the imagined drama or chooses to be a quiet observer, but even as an observer the subject is active in the sense that it is so by active choice. When Jung writes about active imagination, he stresses the word *active* in order to distinguish it from passive fantasy. Both words in active imagination are important – it is imagination and also active, not passive.

Jung's Discovery of Active Imagination as a Method for Psychological Development

It is necessary to look at how Jung came upon active imagination as a method for promoting the individual process, used it on himself, and then applied it in his clinical work with patients. Shortly before his relationship with Freud came to an end, he wrote a book titled *Symbols and Transformations of the Libido*. There, he discussed and analyzed a series of fantasies of a young woman named Frank Miller that had been published in a Swiss psychiatric journal. Basically, he amplified the images of Miss Miller using mythology from many different traditions and parts of the world. He also studied a broad spectrum of literature in order to amplify the deeper meanings of the fantasies Frank Miller had inscribed in her diary. In the first chapter, Jung writes about two types of thinking: fantasy thinking and directed thinking. Fantasy thinking is what Miller used in her productions, whereas directed thinking is the more logical, rational, and scientific type of thinking that Jung used in his discussion of the material. Jung was trained as a scientist and medical doctor, and when he began his research he assumed that directed thinking was far superior to fantasy thinking. Fantasy thinking was considered immature, like what children do when playing with their toys. It is generally considered to be inferior compared to the directed thinking adults employ in their work and daily life. Jung, however, reflected further on the meaning embedded in fantasies and studied them from a deeper psychological perspective, which he would later call archetypal. He came to a new appreciation of fantasy thinking and became fascinated by its profound psychological meaning. In fact, he found that it expresses a kind of psychological truth that directed thinking cannot attain. He discovered the psychological value of images.

This would have monumental consequences for his later psychological theory.

Shortly after the publication of that book, he and Freud ended their personal relationship, and Jung resigned from his positions in the International Psychoanalytic Association. Jung states in *Memories, Dreams, Reflections* that at this time in his life (he was 38 years old), he felt disoriented, and didn't know what direction to take in his life and professional career. He knew that directed thinking and trying to figure it out rationally would not be of much help, so he decided to try an experiment and do what Miss Miller had done, namely to engage fantasy thinking. What is it like to think and yet not use the ego's directed thinking function to solve an existential problem? This was his first question. This experiment resulted in a major turning point that Jung had not anticipated. He discovered active imagination as an agent of transformation. He had set out to discover for himself what it means to think with imagination, and he discovered himself. It was a dramatic journey into and through the inner world.

This experiment was preceded by a number of important dreams that Jung had in the months leading up to his active imagination experiment. He surmised that by using his imagination, he could unlock the meaning of these dreams that he had not been able to interpret using rational methods. Jung begins the story by recalling a dream he had a year or so before beginning the fantasy experiment. In the dream, he's sitting at a round table in his home, and suddenly, a white bird enters the room, sits on the table, and then magically turns into a little girl. Jung is fascinated. She is very charming, so he speaks to her. Then suddenly, she turns back into a white bird and flies out the window and disappears. When he asks someone in the dream: "Where did the little girl go? Where does she live, that white bird?" the answer came back, "She lives in the land of the dead."[1] Jung didn't understand what this meant. Who is this little girl that's also a bird? Where is the land of the dead? What does this all mean?

A year later, in November 1913, Jung made the decision to spend some time in his study every evening after his day's work and dinner with his family in his home in Kusnacht. He set aside a particular time to sit alone in his study and concentrate on this experiment, using fantasy thinking to see where it would lead. He started by opening his mind and, in his imagination, calling out the window overlooking Lake Zurich:

> My soul where are you? Do you hear me? I speak, I call you – are you there? I have returned. I am here again. I have shaken the dust of all the lands from my feet, and I have come to you. I am with you. After long years of long wandering, I have come to you again.[2]

He then simply sat there, maybe an hour or two every evening for several months, and let his imagination explore the inner world that opened up to him. He wanted to find "the land of the dead", his soul, the hidden depths of the psyche. His imagination led him to discover for himself the answers he sought.

Active imagination is an experience, and the knowledge that is acquired by using this method is what might be called Gnosis.

At first, the way inward was very slow and difficult for Jung. For several nights, nothing happened and nothing appeared in his imagination. He waited somewhat impatiently. During this period, as Jung wrote in his notebooks (the *Black Books*), it was as though he were in the desert – dry and barren – and nothing appeared when he called out to his soul. There was no activity at all. Fortunately, he persisted and continued to wait. Finally, a figure whom he calls his soul speaks to him. Only on the twelfth night, he writes, "The spirit of the depths opened my eyes and I caught a glimpse of the inner things, the world of my soul."[3] It was a matter of endurance, like journeying through the desert.

Looking around in this space of his imagination, he suddenly finds himself on the floor of a cave, ankle-deep in mud. Now he could become active by exploring the interior of the cave. This is the beginning of his *active* imagination. As he looks around, he sees a luminous red stone sitting on top of a rock. He approaches to take a closer look, and as he does so, he begins to hear voices shrieking. As he takes the crystal in his hand, he sees a hole in the rock and peers into the underworld. He hears a stream of rushing water deep under the surface of the cave. Jung is astonished by the sounds and images and is surprised by what is happening in his imagination. (Surprise is a very important feature of active imagination – something happens that the subject does not expect. The ego is not in charge, and the unconscious images are showing autonomy.) As Jung peers into the depths, he sees something very disturbing: the bloody head of a man, and a dead body is floating in the water. He then sees a large dark scarab and a radiant sun shining up through the dark waters. Blood suddenly starts pouring out of the hole. Jung had no idea what this experience meant or how to interpret it. He simply made a record in his journal, writing down everything he saw, thought, and felt. But the meaning was unclear to him. Yet from his studies of mythology, he knew that this was part of the process that is classically called a Nekyia, a journey into the underworld. The parallel between the psychological descent into the unconscious using active imagination and the mythological accounts of this journey is obvious.

We have to keep in mind when reading *Liber Novus* that Jung, unlike Dante for instance, did not have a master guide to lead him or shed light on the meaning of the process he was undergoing. In fact, he was quite alone and at times became worried about where this experiment was taking him. Would he end up with a mental breakdown? Would he "throw a schizophrenia?" as it was called in the Burghölzli Klinik, he wondered anxiously. He was an experienced psychiatrist and had seen what mental illness looks like. He worried about the possibility of a latent psychosis lurking in his unconscious that might burst through the walls of his ego-consciousness and render him temporarily incapable of functioning. He had seen patients in the hospital with the kind of fantasies he was experiencing in his private office. It was a serious concern.

On the other hand, he was pleased that his imagination was working so energetically, that something indeed was happening, and that he was being surprised. His imagination was coming to life, becoming interesting and dynamic. Reflecting on his options, he decided to continue his experiment.

A week after his visit to the cave, he comes upon a scene in which he meets two figures: an old man who looks like one of the ancient prophets and a beautiful young woman who is blind. They are accompanied by a black serpent. With this encounter, the first major episode in *Liber Novus* unfolds. The prophet introduces himself as Elijah and the woman as Salome. Jung is astonished, and a fascinating narrative develops over the course of their interactions and conversations. The episode lasts for five sessions of active imagination, December 21–25, 1913. Jung discovers that they also live in the Land of the Dead, which is where the girl in his earlier dream was from and which he had set out to find when he began his experiment with imagination. This territory is what he would call in his theoretical writings on psychology "the collective unconscious". It is where myths come from. He has found the source, and he is discovering his personal myth.

Who are these two people? Salome and Elijah are biblical figures, so they've long since been dead, and yet they are still very much alive in this land where they currently live. Jung is discovering that the Land of the Dead is cultural history and now a part of the collective unconscious. That long-ago past is still alive and active within the psyche. This would lead him to argue that in the unconscious time does not exist as it does in consciousness. The distinction among past, present, and future breaks down in the unconscious. Everything is present at once. As we observe Jung's behaviour and how he interacts with these figures, we see that he remains himself an educated European man of the twentieth century. He remains very much himself in his questioning, arguing, and thinking. He doesn't become fictionalized or different from his usual waking personality. In his active imagination, he is engaging with figures who, while they are a part of himself in the sense of belonging to his inner world, yet are unfamiliar to him and represent attitudes and viewpoints other than his conscious ones. In *Liber Novus*, we can observe how Jung, as he practices active imagination over several years, gradually undergoes a profound transformation. Not only does he change and evolve, however, but the figures with which he interacts also evolve. There is a mutual transformation process going on in which all parts of the psyche are affected because of the dialogue and the interaction taking place between them.

At a certain point, Jung was so impressed by what was happening to him inwardly that he decided to create what we now know as *The Red Book*, which he titled *Liber Novus* (*The New Book*). Jung thought deeply and over a long period of time about the meaning of his active imagination narrative. Besides reflecting on the psychological meaning for himself personally, he also introduced active imagination as a therapeutic method to his patients. In 1916, some three years after he began his experiment, he delivered a paper to his students and colleagues at the Psychology Club titled "The Transcendent Function".[4] There, he describes the practice of active imagination and presents the result of this work as the construction of a bridge between ego-consciousness and the unconscious. The meaning of "transcendent" in this term is that it rises above the abyss between the two sides of the psyche. The "transcendent function" allows the conscious mind to go beyond the limits of directed rational thinking and connects the ego to another realm of the psyche, thereby delivering what could be called intuitive knowledge, or "gnosis". Jung came to realize that directed thinking cannot connect the ego to the unconscious. It can study the effects of the unconscious, as Jung and his colleagues did in the Word Association Studies and as Freud did in his psychoanalysis, but its range of experience is limited to consciousness. Active imagination can take the subject further into what Henry Corbin, following Jung and expanding on the topic of active imagination from his studies in Sufism, called the *Mundus Imaginalis*.

Active Imagination in Jungian Psychoanalysis

Imagine going to Jung for analysis, stepping into his office, and meeting him. The first session is introductory: You tell your story, list your complaints and problems, and Jung listens carefully but does not say much. Then, he encourages you to do two things before you come to the next session: to record your dreams and to begin practicing active imagination. If he said this to you, it would be a real compliment—he would be estimating that you are capable of doing this inner work. He would have made a very quick evaluation and diagnosis of your psychological stability and capacity. By the end of the session, he is in effect saying, "You are ready to work and do analysis with me." This would begin an extraordinary period of working in introversion.

You would be engaged in a lot of work between sessions if you were in analysis with Jung. It isn't only taking place in the hour of analysis; it's ongoing, intensive work between the hours of analysis. Jung worked in this way with most of his patients in his later life. His clients were mostly mature people, some of them well advanced into the second half of life. If he worked with you in this thoroughly engaged way, he would be assuming that you did not need to do the work that's so necessary in the first half of life: building a persona, getting into your life, and becoming independent of your family of origin, creating a strong ego. He would assume that you've done that already. Many people who worked with Jung in analysis would go into this type of total immersion for a relatively short period of time. They would come to Zurich and do analysis with him for a couple of months and then return home. Many of his patients lived in other countries.

While they were with him, they exerted themselves intensively in an introverted way in order to experience and build up an inner world by making contact with figures of the unconscious through working with their dreams and engaging in active imagination. It was a very special time in their lives as Jung assisted and guided them in the discovery of their inner depths.

Once they were advanced in active imagination and working with their dreams, they could carry on these activities without necessarily having to be in analysis. After they left their residency in Switzerland and went back home, the work they began with Jung could continue. Active imagination helped them to become independent of the analyst. It facilitated an ongoing process. They had developed certain skills and the ability to be in a creative and fruitful relationship with their unconscious independently. Typically, Jung's patients would begin their active imagination work when they came to see him and then continue doing it perhaps for the rest of their lives, perhaps returning to see him occasionally. During these reunions with Jung, they might review some of the experiences they had in the meantime. But Jung felt that learning to do active imagination freed them from the transference and from dependency on him. It gave them the ability to continue their inner work on their own, when they were not actively in analysis with him.

Joseph Henderson, an American, came to Zurich as a young man in the 1920s and worked with Jung for a period of time. After he finished his training, which took place between Zurich and London, he moved to San Francisco and eventually founded the Jung Institute there with his friend and colleague Joseph Wheelwright. Joseph Henderson once told me a bit about his experience in Kusnacht. He stayed in a hotel not far from Jung's home and walked there for his sessions several times a week. In the early morning, he said, he would come out on the hotel terrace and see other people sitting there working on their dreams or quietly doing active imagination. He said that's how you could tell which of the hotel guests were working with Jung. If they were sitting on the terrace writing in their journals, painting a picture, or with their eyes closed and obviously doing active imagination, they were Jung's patients. These people were preparing for their analytic session with Jung. Henderson told me that it was inconceivable to work with Jung and not be engaged in active imagination. It was a basic method regularly employed by Jung in analysis.

Jung discusses several analytic cases in his published writings and seminars that include extensive active imagination content. In *The Visions Seminar*, he looks at the active imagination material of Christiana Morgan, an American woman who came for sessions in the 1920s and later returned to Boston, where, with Henry Murray, she created the Thematic Apperception Test (TAT). He devotes a major section of his book *Psychology and Alchemy* to a series of dreams and active imaginations by the physicist Wolfgang Pauli, who came to him for analysis in the 1930s. And he writes a major essay titled "A Study in the Process of Individuation" on the active imaginations and paintings of Kristine Mann, an American psychiatrist who came to study with him in the 1920s and continued with intermittent frequency until her death in the 1940s.

As an example of the therapeutic effects of active imagination, the case of Wolfgang Pauli is instructive. Pauli was a professor at ETH Zurich, where Jung was also a professor at the time. His father, who was a professor in Vienna, suggested that he consult with Jung about the troubles he was having in his personal life. Pauli realized that he needed help, so he came to Jung for analysis. Jung interviewed him and decided it would be better if he began by working with a female colleague and student of his because Pauli was having a lot of difficulties in his relationships with women. Second, both Pauli and Jung were professors at the same university, and it probably would have been difficult to separate roles. So, Jung referred him to Dr. Erna Rosenbaum, who took over the analysis of Pauli. He was in analysis with Rosenbaum for some nine months, during which time he produced an impressive series of dreams and active imaginations, which he then offered to Jung for his research purposes. It is these that Jung analyzes in his commentary. After his analysis with Rosenbaum, he continued in analysis with Jung for some 18 months, after which their relationship changed and continued in the form of correspondence and occasional meetings to discuss theoretical topics and occasionally Pauli's dreams.

About 18 years later, in 1953, Pauli produced a paper called "The Piano Lesson", which is an active imagination of about ten pages in length. It shows Pauli creating a balance and harmony between two parts within himself. In this active imagination, he finds a way to bring together his rational, scientific, and brilliant intelligence with his emotional life, with his anima world and the unconscious. He uses the metaphor of the piano with white and black keys working together to create a single piece of music. It could be said that through the use of active imagination and working with his dreams, Pauli was able to achieve a very considerable level of balance and integration of the opposites. It was this inner harmony that was crucial for his life and for his work.

Jung found Pauli's dreams and active imagination material fascinating because Pauli was such a gifted man, committed to recording his dreams in detail, and exceptional at working with his images and visions. He was dedicated to active imagination, as the record shows. In Pauli's case, we can see how dreams and active imaginations move together in a steady and clear direction toward what Jung called the synthesis of the psyche and the development of a transcendent function. One of the things that Pauli realized as a result of his analysis was how therapeutic this was for his daily life. As long as he stayed in contact with his unconscious by observing his dreams and working in active imagination, he felt emotionally stable, enriched, and balanced. He continued doing this for the rest of his life.

Kristine Mann presents a complementary case. She was an American woman who came to Jung for analysis in the 1920s, when she was about 55 years old. Mann was an accomplished single professional woman, a psychiatrist with a practice in New York City, who felt a need to work with her unconscious in a different way than had been available to her. She felt stuck. She came to Jung hoping to find a way forward in her life and her individuation process. Jung comments on about 20 pictures that Mann painted while in analysis with him and afterward in "A Study in the Process of Individuation", which was published after her death.

The first picture that she brought to Jung when she came to him for analysis shows a woman stuck in rocks. The second picture shows a lightning strike, which frees a boulder from the rocks. Release and freedom from oppression are represented in this picture. Mann practiced active imagination by painting. This is one of the ways that active imagination can be done: hand to paper with a brush, putting the images on a surface so they can be seen instead of holding them in imagination. When Mann brought these pictures to Jung, they would discuss them as products of active imagination. She would tell him what they meant to her and how they came about. At one point, she said that she had decided not to follow "reason" but to let her "eyes" lead the way and tell her how the images would be presented. In this way, she would be surprised by the picture that emerged.

The picture series that she produced represents her individuation process in images. When she returned to New York after working with Jung for several months in Switzerland, she continued active imagination in painting. She would if possible return to Switzerland in the summers and resume her work with Jung for several weeks. Over the course of about 20 years, she produced a series of impressive paintings, many of them in the form of a mandala. Jung writes in his commentary on these pictures about the process of individuation that he sees moving forward step by step in these images. This was her form of active imagination, and it was transformative.

Precautions for the Use of Active Imagination

There are a number of precautions one needs to consider before using active imagination. One has to be aware of psychological conditions and degree of psychopathology. Active imagination can become a very powerful and disruptive method because it stimulates the unconscious, and images emerge in the process that can be disturbing, as one can see clearly in Jung's *Liber Novus*. If the ego isn't strong enough to contain the affects released and work with the images as they emerge, one can become overwhelmed by what Jung called a latent psychosis. Analysts will typically work with their clients for a period of time before they decide whether it's appropriate to introduce active imagination as a method. With some clients, one would never use it either because of psychopathology or lack of sufficient ego development or inappropriate timing, given what is happening in the client's life at the time.

Another rule in active imagination is not to use known persons as active imagination characters. It would be a misuse of active imagination to try to influence other people through a type of "magical intervention". If by chance a known person pops up in active imagination, the advice is to find a replacement for that person. For instance, if Mr. Z, who is someone whom I find distasteful and is a kind of shadow figure for me, comes into my active imagination, I recognize him and try to find a similar imaginal character to represent the same shadow qualities. I can then go ahead and dialogue with him.

Types of Active Imagination

There are a variety of modes one can use in active imagination. The instructions here could be called the classical form: You create a clear space in your mind, wait for whatever appears, if it moves follow it, and so on. Then there is the modality that Kristine Mann used: drawing and painting. Some people use clay modeling or sculpting. There is also active imagination in movement, where the body leads the way in active imagination. This is practiced by some Jungian analysts and is called "authentic movement." And then, of course, there is sandplay, which is practiced by many therapists worldwide. For this, one places miniature objects in a tray of sand and creates a scene from which a narrative emerges. Today one might also consider making a film as a form of active imagination.

Starting Points for Active Imagination

Active imagination can start in a variety of ways. It can begin with a dream. If a dream is unfinished upon awakening, or if there is something in the dream that the dreamer would like to explore further, or if there is a figure in the dream to engage with further, active imagination can be used to dream the dream onward.

Active imagination may also begin with a mood or a feeling. If you were going to make a movie to represent this feeling, what would it be about, and what role would you play? Starting with a feeling or a mood, perhaps in imagination you find yourself alone beside a lake and someone comes toward you – you engage that person in dialogue.

Some Tips for the Practicing of Active Imagination

To begin, there is a starting point, a first session. One needs to make a quiet and free mental space for imagination. As I have said, active imagination is not daydreaming or a matter of falling into a fantasy that pops into consciousness. Active imagination is a deliberate undertaking, and one has to prepare for it. Begin by setting aside 30 minutes in a physical place free of outside disturbance: no telephone calls, no messages, no conversation.

Tip 1: "Let It Happen!" (Geschenlassen, Wu Wei)

The first rule is simple: Just let it happen. In German, the word to describe this type of activity is the verb, *geschenlassen*. When Jung studied and commented on the Chinese alchemical text *The Secret of the Golden Flower*, he discovered that this has an equivalent in the Chinese language: *wu wei*. It's a type of active passivity: active in that it is a choice made by the awake subject (the ego); passive in that it means "do nothing, wait". This is the first instruction Jung received from his soul. She whispered to him, "Wait". It's a simple instruction, but it can be agonizing to carry out: "I heard the cruel word. Torment belongs to the desert,"[5] Jung writes in *Liber Novus*.

At first, you might have to wait patiently for quite a time until something starts to happen in your imagination. It is not easy to empty the busy mind of the thoughts that preoccupy it. It's a discipline. Spurious thoughts keep intruding, and it's a challenge to let them go. The idea is to create a blank screen in your mind in which you're thinking of nothing, seeing nothing, feeling nothing – it's just empty space. In some forms of meditation, this is the final goal. For active imagination, it's the beginning, a prerequisite.

To do this, it's helpful if your body is relaxed. In some meditation practices, people sit on a cushion with their legs crossed or folded. There is also the so-called walking meditation. The main thing is to calm your conscious mind, to empty it of its concerns and preoccupations. When complexes, worries, or thoughts from everyday life intrude, just let them go and clear the space. This is what we see Jung doing at the beginning of *Liber Novus*. Simply and patiently wait for something to appear, not forcing it, not trying to summon an image. This is the initial session. Later, there will be a change in how to begin a session of active imagination, but at the beginning, start with emptiness.

Marie-Louise von Franz, who was one of Jung's outstanding students and wrote a good deal about active imagination, including a book titled *Alchemical Active Imagination*, once told the story of a client whom she advised to do some active imagination. She gave him the basic instructions as outlined above, and when the client came to her for his session the next week, she asked: "Did you do the exercise?" He replied: "I tried, but nothing happened. Nothing came to me. I didn't see anything." She suggested he try again the following week: "Do the same thing. Clear your mind, make an empty space and wait. See what comes to you." The next week the report was the same. He said he tried to do the active imagination and sat quietly for half an hour. He waited, cleared his mind, but nothing came. This went on for weeks and weeks, and it was always the same story. He was a very patient man, so he continued faithfully to try. Then, one week he came in really excited and said: "I saw something!" She asked, "What did you see?" He said he was sitting quietly as usual in front of his window at home when, all of a sudden, he saw the image of a goat outside the window. The goat was just standing there and looking off into the distance. She said, "That's great. Now it's begun." He told her that he didn't like goats very much, and he wished it had been something else. Dr. Von Franz said, "Just stay with what you see."

Tip 2: "Receive Whatever Comes"

This brings us to the second rule. Von Franz's client would rather have had something more interesting than a goat. He lived in the countryside of Switzerland where goats are rather commonplace and not very interesting. Maybe he would rather have seen an eagle or a mountain lion. But he was instructed to stay with what came to him. This is an essential rule. We can remember Jung's experience from *The Red Book* where he describes going into the cave and seeing something horrible, something he would not have invited or wanted in any way. Yet he had to accept what was offered in his imagination. We all have an inner editor; an attitude or judge of what's noble, what's base, what's worthy, and what's unworthy. We have to put that editor aside and simply receive whatever comes – the first thing that arrives and reveals itself in the imagination.

This rule sets active imagination apart and makes it different from meditation practices that have a program or guided imagery. For instance, in guided meditation, you may begin by thinking about a particular scene from a particular text, and in the second meditation, you may meditate on a particular figure or deity. There are instructions for each of these. Active imagination is not like this. Once you've made yourself comfortable, cleared your mind of distracting thoughts, and something appears to you in your space of imagination, don't judge it. Just receive it, accept it, and stay with it.

This is the instruction that Von Franz gave to her client. She said, "You've seen a goat outside the window? Stay with it – what does it do? Watch it. Pay attention and see what happens." When the client came back the next week for his session, she asked him what happened. The client said that nothing happened, the goat just stayed where he was the week before. She again encouraged him saying, "Well, stay with it during the week, keep doing it every day, watch him, stay with the image, see what happens." He came back the following week, and it was the same story – nothing happened. This went on for weeks and weeks. He was patient and kept looking out the window – the goat was still there. But nothing happened beyond that.

Then suddenly in the middle of the night, Von Franz's phone rang, and she picked up the receiver. It was this client on the other end of the line. "Dr. Von Franz, I'm going crazy! You have to admit me to the mental hospital. I'm losing my mind." She said to him on the phone: "Can you wait till the morning? I'll see you early. Come to my office at 7.00 a.m. We'll have an emergency session. You can tell me what's happening, and we'll see if you need to be hospitalized. I'll take care of it. But can you wait until morning?" He said he would wait. When he arrived at 7.00 a.m. the next morning, she let him into her consulting room. "What happened? What's the matter? Tell me what's going on." He said when he was doing his active imagination yesterday, looking out the window as usual, he saw the head of the goat. All of a sudden, the goat moved his head and looked right at him. "I'm sure I'm going crazy. I can't control my mind. That goat is just doing whatever it wants." Von Franz laughed and said that's what is supposed to happen in active imagination. "Now you have something happening and you can interact with that goat. Active imagination is beginning now."

Tip 3: "If It Moves, Follow It"

This introduces the third rule of active imagination. *If it moves, follow it* and stay with that movement in the imagination. This brings in not only the rule of acceptance – staying with whatever comes – but it also brings in the rule of the active ego engaging with autonomous figures in the imagination, which seem to have a life and will of their own. In this stage of active imagination, it's important that the ego, the "I" in the story, maintains its usual attitudes and feelings. Subjects need to enter the story that's developing with the full reality of who they are and act as though the dialogue and scene is really happening in front of them. That's the difference between active imagination and passive fantasy. In passive fantasy, you just watch what's happening. In active imagination, you enter into it and engage with it as though it were a real, physical, dramatic event happening in front of you and around you.

Jung tells the story of a patient, a young man, who came to him with an account of an active imagination he had done between sessions. The young man said that in his active imagination, he was with his fiancée who was skating on the ice of a nearby lake. He was standing at the edge of the lake watching. Suddenly, the ice broke, and she fell into the ice-cold water and was screaming for help, and it looked as if she were drowning. Jung exclaimed, "Oh no! What did you do?" The young man admitted with embarrassment that he just stood passively and watched the scene in front of him as if it were a movie. Jung asked, "What would you do if this was really happening?" He said that if it were really happening, he would call for help and would jump into the water to try to save her. Jung said: "Well, that's exactly what you should do in active imagination. Be yourself as much as you possibly can, as you would be if this event were taking place in the physical world around you." The point is that there is strong ego-involvement in active imagination. This is not passive fantasy. The ego allows the story to unfold, but at the same time, the subject is also an actor in the scene that's being played out in the imagination.

These are the basic rules of active imagination: Let go and empty the mind; receive whatever comes; if it moves follow it; and then interact genuinely with it. If you follow these basic rules, you're sure to have success in practicing active imagination.

If you wish to try active imagination, follow these rules. Set aside 20 to 30 minutes every day for a week and make an attempt to begin active imagination. You can set a timer, and after about 20 minutes of practicing your active imagination, write down in a journal exactly what happened. The next day, pick up where you left it the day before. Go back into the scene and continue from there. If you do this regularly for a month, you will have the beginning of a stable inner world that you can visit and receive the benefits of active imagination for the rest of your life. This sounds like a big promise; it actually depends on your determination and patience. You have it within your psyche to exercise this function of imagination and to use it actively. This opens you up to an experience of the inner world and a connection to the unconscious.

As well as following the rules, it's also important not to interpret the active imagination while it is happening. Just let it unfold and record it. Understanding the meaning will come later, but meanwhile don't use your cognitive functions of interpretation, or it will block further development. Active imagination is an experience of image, story, and feeling. You'll find that you can become very emotional while doing active imagination. That's why it's wise to put a time limit on it; 20 or 30 minutes a day is really enough. Don't get overly involved, and always keep conscious control over this imaginative activity in which you're engaging.

In experimenting with active imagination, you should write down everything that you experience, see, hear, or feel. Be sure to include it in your journal, because you want to be able to go back and trace your steps later. Do not be tempted to interpret too much as you go. Wait until the process has been very well established before looking into the meaning. Just stay with the symbols and figures and keep working with them. When the series has run its course, you can try to interpret it using suitable psychological concepts.

Jung also speaks of the ethical obligation that comes along with messages from the Self. Active imagination is a method for listening to the hints offered by the Self for becoming more conscious of the whole length and breadth of the psyche, including the opposites contained in the Self. It is the ego that bears the responsibility for integrating the messages received into everyday life. In active imagination, for example, one might receive a hint of vocation. This is to be taken up seriously by the ego, thought through carefully and with ethical awareness, and then built into the direction one's future takes. This is what Jung speaks of as the "ethical aspect" of working with the unconscious. It is the next step after the "aesthetic aspect", which is the simple notation and appreciation of the images and energies experienced in active imagination or in dreams. For this reason, it is not advisable to practice active imagination as a kind of entertainment or psychic make-believe activity. Realizations of the Self carry an ethical responsibility.

Notes

1 C.G. Jung, *Memories, Dreams, Reflections*, p. 172. Author's summary.
2 C.G. Jung, *The Red Book: Liber Novus*, Reader's Edition, p. 127.
3 Ibid., p. 147.
4 C.G. Jung, "The Transcendent Function", CW 8.
5 Ibid., p. 141.

References

Jung, C.G. (1961). *Memories, Dreams, Reflections*. New York: Vintage.
Jung, C.G. (2009). *The Red Book: Liber Novus*. A Reader's Edition. New York: W.W. Norton & Company.

Chapter 3

Active Imagination and the Process of Individuation

Federico De Luca Comandini
Translated by Robert Mercurio

The Fork in the Road

Viewed in their entirety, the works of Jung show clearly just how central active imagination is to one's whole psychological process. His essays, starting from "The Transcendent Function" written in 1916 right through to "Mysterium co-niunctionis", dating from 1955, are peppered with references to the importance of this practice. At first glance, we might be struck by the fact that the *Collected Works* do not contain an essay fully dedicated to this topic, but on closer exami-nation, it would seem that Jung preferred to avoid dealing with the process of imagination in treatises of a technical or theoretical nature. There may be a num-ber of reasons for this, but the principal one seems to be the need to protect the intimate symbolic sense of imaginative work from intellectualistic abstraction on the one hand, and from overly practical "how to do it" explanations on the other hand. Jung chose to scatter throughout his works a great number of references to the role that active imagination plays in one's process of psychological growth, entrusting the task of handing on the sense and meaning of this practice to inter-personal, oral tradition so as to leave the "map" of the path of individuation dis-cretely and reservedly veiled. As we know, Jung was not in the habit of utilizing the literary form of the "case study", nor would a text of that sort have been able to grasp and convey the imaginative movements that contribute to one's personal symbolic transformation. The sort of experience that Jung proposes through the use of active imagination goes beyond the scope of the usual sort of communica-tion used among the members of psychotherapeutic groups, even those who are particularly attentive to analytical questions as such. Jung keeps his distance from all of this so as to be able to freely express individual forms of psychological creativity.

I would like to hazard a somewhat unorthodox metaphor: psychotherapy might be seen as a rocket which is launched into psychic space out of the need to find so-lutions to situations of personal suffering. It rises above the earth's atmosphere (the force of gravity of our concrete daily existence) in search of a deeper and healthier sense of meaning. The first phase of this rocket's journey could be called the "ana-lytical setting" where the pilot and crew members (or the therapist and passenger/

DOI: 10.4324/9781003411369-3

client, if you prefer) are engaged in the common task of recognizing and respecting the rocket trajectory that needs to be followed.

Once the rocket has cleared the earth's atmosphere and freed itself from its gravitational pull, part of the rocket is discarded and from this point onward our passenger will be travelling on their own, facing their therapeutic journey without the help of assistants in the cockpit. But on closer examination, we see that he or she is not alone, but in the company of the images which the unconscious provides in a manner similar to the dreaming process. Out of the collaboration among these various figures, a new crew comes to life, and the goal of the voyage changes into a search aimed at the psychological individuation of the passenger. This second phase of the rocket's voyage could be called the "imaginal setting".

In more straightforward language, putting aside metaphors, it is clear that active imagination goes well beyond what normally happens in the consulting room, and at this point the analytical journey becomes a deep search for meaning in a way which corresponds to the individual characteristics of the client. This in no way deprives interpersonal relationships of their value and importance nor does it diminish the importance of sharing in the context of the therapeutic relationship. Our lives are, after all, filled with hard facts and real people. Naturally all of this remains in the client's life and continues to have its importance.

The absolutely individual element which characterizes one's personal search for meaning takes us well above and beyond anything we could hope to define statistically. Each person is the unrepeatable sum total of the persons who live around and within the subject. This mysterious reality cannot be reduced to a mere portrait of the social or familial context of the client's life and from this point of view the work of psychological differentiation represents the development of life-giving perspectives which are ethically fundamental to an individual's life and through which the genuine inner voice of each person's existence can make itself heard. This is precisely the approach which leads to the experience of living a complete and fulfilling life.

Man is naturally a "social animal" but the psychological evolution of an individual brings her or him face to face with a basic question: what does the meaning of existence grow out of? Collective consciousness, in all of its various and, at times, contradictory manifestations, is sorely lacking in terms of the ability to propose an answer to this question. From a psychological perspective, the weakening and the emptying of the divine images which held sway in this arena have left a void which is indeed hard to fill. Jung warned us many years ago that the necessity of filling this void exposed human consciousness to the risk of inflating the worth and importance of the immanent aspects of life and we, as "social animals" tend to search for meaning in numbers, statistics, algorithms, thus losing sight of the complex totality which we are part of. Here we encounter a fork in the road of life, and the risk of heading down the road of statistics and numbers is serious.

In choosing the other path, a human being engages in a process of ethical maturation which can lead her or him to step back from and out of the sense of identity which is entrusted to one's numerical place in the labyrinth of social projections and where the value of an individual is measured statistically. Here *meaning* and *identity* are expressed in terms of the various social roles we fill: *voter* or *customer*. The "other" path, the path of psychological individuation, presents us with a chance to find a symbolic orientation which in turn can lead us to the discovery of a *meaning* which is far more trustworthy than what the concrete facts of life can give us. Theoretically, the prospect may be enticing but it involves the hard work of deep psychological searching and a precise form of psychological formation. Active imagination corresponds to just what we have been describing here: a personal, individual practice, carried out outside of the analytical setting and which gives direction to one's psychological search on the basis of one's personal sense of meaning. It will take an individual beyond the confines of what had been discovered and consolidated in the work done with the analyst.

The Archetypal Dimension of the Transference

Considerations that have to do with the conclusion of analysis inevitably take us to the question of what happens to the analytical *transference* and the prickly question of how it can be "dissolved". The whole psychoanalytical tradition has not been able to offer a convincing answer to the question and often it has opted to simply avoid or ignore it. As we know, it was fundamental for Jung that a person who chose to embark on the journey of individuation with him be able to undertake independently a personal imaginative process which in turn would indicate the degree of psychological autonomy the patient was capable of assuming. This should be, for all of us, the principal objective of the therapy we do.

The debate over the question as to whether analysis is terminable or interminable often risks becoming messy and confused in the way it places at the centre of everything the difficulties a patient may have in elaborating the closing of the analytical relationship. At times the debate seems to dissolve in a simple *in caudum velenum*. Freud's references to the *transference neurosis* have to do mainly with the resistance a patient may feel in the face of the need to begin standing and progressing on his or her own two feet, without the assistance of the analyst. Naturally, there is something to be said for this approach, but the psychoanalytical tradition seems to have one-sidedly placed too much emphasis on the role of parental projections and the way they contribute to creating an infantile *impasse* in the client. The collective thinking associated with any group will inevitably lead its members to identify the sliver in the eye of another while overlooking the beam in its own eye. This keeps us from having a balanced view of the whole question, and if the analyst slips into one of the many forms of abuse of his or her role, the whole therapeutic undertaking suffers. For this reason, it seems to be important to examine that other pole in the therapeutic relationship: what role and responsibility has the analyst in this whole question?

The phenomenon of the transference, regardless of the specific interpretation we might attribute to that term, grows out of a desire for transformation, a desire that needs to be recognized and supported in analysis. Direct experience of the force of the unconscious and the psychic images that are delved into with the analyst will create a quantity of energy that spills out over and beyond the questions that are worked on in the sessions as such. If the therapy is really working, both parties will be intensely involved, for better or worse, because a new sort of relationship both with another person and with the parts within each of the parties, will be taking shape in a way which previously could not have transpired. Feeling isolated and cut off is the one most common trait found in nearly every form of psychic suffering, and the transference offers a chance of experiencing a sense of togetherness not only thanks to the human relationship with the analyst but also the connection between what one was and what one really is, and even more, what one could be. From this point of view, the desire for transformation is more than a simple wish for change but rather, thanks to the connection with the unconscious, becomes a dynamic flow that reorganizes and enlivens the whole personality including one's present reality and what is yet to be realized in life.

If the transference implies all that we have suggested here, then we need to ask ourselves a further question: how could an analytical relationship end on a positive note unless we somehow provide a means for that desire for transformation to be taken away, out of the consulting room? If a client feels he or she has no way of cherishing and developing that transformative experience, he or she will naturally resist ending the therapy. For many people, it is not enough to have obtained good results in terms of adaptive skills, the remission of bothersome symptoms of a widening of consciousness. Feeling better and more in tune with life after an analysis carried out correctly may not be adequate especially if there is no viable way of keeping the desire for transformation alive and functioning. If this is not taken seriously into consideration, the risks of inflation or depression will be just around the corner since these distortions are inevitable when psychological creativity finds no symbolic container and is simply discharged one-sidedly onto the concrete world. Jung refers to this very danger with the phrase "regressive reconstitution of the Persona". It will then be the task and responsibility of the therapist to start laying the foundation for this delicate passage by providing the tools which are necessary for carrying on, in a personal way, the psychological work begun in analysis, after analysis itself. If the "resolution of the transference" does not have a dynamic character which opens the way to further development, the client will be trapped in a guilt-ridden situation in which they may feel that the difficulty in dealing with this transition is their own fault or that they need to consult yet another analyst. If the analyst does not carefully take into consideration the problem of "what happens after" analysis, he or she will simply contribute to the creation of this short circuit. The explanation of the "transference neurosis" will be dumped onto the shoulders of the client while the analyst, whose shadow risks being mystified, will remain beyond criticism.

There is, quite honestly, something scandalous in this way of proceeding; active imagination on the other hand can open up, in a serious and rigorous manner, new post-analytical perspectives. Everything that transpired during the analytical sessions, if it has indeed been able to reach fruition, can be seen as preparation for further personal developments of the client's individual psychological *opus*. Jung himself was wont to say that one needed to know how to meet the unconscious alone, on one's own.

Lack of Awareness, Curiosity and Various Concretistic Views

Despite the richness of this practice, active imagination has for years been forgotten or neglected both in terms of research into the topic and as an element in the formation of analysts. As mentioned earlier, the simple fact that the nature and importance of this practice depend largely on personal communication has no doubt contributed to this and might explain why, even though large numbers of people have been attracted to Jung's analytical psychology in the last few decades, relatively few have deepened their knowledge of active imagination. Naturally the lack of recognition of the importance of the psychology of the unconscious in our public institutions has made all of this even worse, and all of those aspects of psychology that are in contrast with a positivistic approach have been relegated to the sidelines. Sadly, even many associations which pledge allegiance to Jung have given precedence to approaches which correspond to collective views and expectations.

The approach and vision offered by Jung may at times seem to replicate both the language and the methodologies of traditional science, but they take us well beyond the claims to exhaustive explanations advanced by the scientific world. Jung's approach integrates in complementary fashion, all of those "humanistic" concerns such as the value of the subjective factor and of the imaginal and affective aspects of life which the hard sciences neglect. Active imagination represents a unique and extreme example of this: it is a basically introverted practice rooted in the subjective feeling life of the person involved. It produces nothing that can be objectively proven and verified using the tools and techniques of the scientific method. Like the interpretative work we do on dreams, it is a symbolic activity, containing both conscious and unconscious elements and which in the end cannot be summed up by any rational explanation. Despite the fact that it occupies a place at the very heart of analytical psychology, it has been, with very few exceptions, completely forgotten for many years.

The publication of Jung's *Red Book* has in many ways changed this situation. It has been hailed as an exceptional event and the book itself, due to the exceptional nature of the text and the surprisingly beautiful and complex images that accompany it, attracted the attention and admiration of people from well beyond the confines of the world of psychology. And now it will no longer be possible to deny the importance of active imagination within Jungian circles. It would seem that the entire world of psychoanalysis can find here stimuli for reflection. And yet, the excessive amount of investigation into the sources and nature of the text make it hard to be genuinely optimistic. Books, articles, seminars and conferences on *The Red Book* which are often devoid of a correct acknowledgement of the real meaning of this work, unfortunately abound.

We should keep in mind that work on *The Red Book* was undertaken by Jung as a project for himself and not to produce something that others could read. It was his very personal psychological diary, a container for his symbolic processes. It contains his experiences of active imagination and, as the laboratory of his internal life, was conceived as something that had to do with him alone. No one could say that Jung had not generously shared and explained his views and recounted his own personal experiences. His *Collected Works*, his autobiography and a plethora of open and candid interviews testify to this fact. It is presumptuous, to say the least, to think we have the right to enter into his most private life, as if we were storming into his bedroom (but isn't that what works and studies on the Sabina Spielrein affair have done?). Collective curiosity is rampant around important and famous individuals, and it demands more and more details, which often invade the privacy we all have a right to. The same is true for Jung. The publication of *The Red Book* understandably aroused embarrassment and perplexity among many members of the family. After all, Jung himself considered the book "private". But now historiographers consider the text not a personal diary but rather a "document" that needs to be examined, studied, evaluated, judged and catalogued.

Now that Jung's experiences of active imagination are there to be read and studied by everyone, we need to reflect on the question of what use we want to make of this. The question is of the utmost importance both in terms of our relationship with Jung and with ourselves. As far as our relationship with Jung is concerned, we obviously need to treat the material he produced with the greatest respect. The imaginative approach that he discovered and developed has meaning and value only on the level of the individual, since it gives unique expression to the unification of the personality and holds the secret symbol of its very existence. Any sort of "psychologization" would be completely inappropriate. The only appropriate and respectful way of approaching material of this nature is to read it while abstaining, both internally and in conversation with others, from any sort of comment or criticism. This is exactly the attitude that must be maintained when one is asked to listen to an example of active imagination, and it is a fundamental principle of Jungian psychology.

Having said all of this, we return to the question of how to evaluate the publication of Jung's *Red Book*. How do we deal with it? As an extraordinary example of the imaginative approach which should encourage us to find *our own imaginative paths* without attempting to imitate or ape what Jung discovered in his symbolic journey.

The Two Phases of the Psychological Process and the Feeling of Togetherness

Having left to Jung that which was and is Jung's, we can now focus on what concerns us in so far as we are personally involved in an ethical confrontation with the unconscious in search of a more meaningful way of living. The heart of the question does not, after all, really have to do with Jung's magnificent *Red Book* but rather with our ability to follow the precious indications found there, that is to carry on our personal search for meaning with the use of active imagination.

From this point of view, it is important to review the important distinction introduced into psychoanalytical circles by analytical psychology. In some of his essays which were written in a popular and very accessible style (such as *The Relations between the Ego and the Unconscious*, 1928) Jung introduced the distinction between what he terms the "analytical-reductive" phase of psychological work and the "synthetic-constructive" phase. These two phases should not of course be understood as chronologically subsequent to one another but rather as two methodological approaches. The "analytical" way of proceeding tends to bring about a conscious recognition of the manifestations of the unconscious in the hopes of counterbalancing the effects of these manifestations and, hopefully, of integrating these contents into the personality. Jung himself admits that from this point of view, his approach follows the paths laid out by Freud and Adler since the goal which the various schools of psychoanalysis have in common consists of the weakening of the disturbing influence of the unconscious along with an explanation of these psychic intrusions. Jung clearly declares that he has no specific approach of his own in this regard, and informs us that at times he utilizes the Freudian psychosexual approach and at other times, on the basis of the needs of the patient, the Adlerian approach centred on questions of power and social recognition. Jung's original contribution emerges in the "synthetic-constructive" phase of the work where the insights gained from the analytical work on the differentiation between conscious and unconscious contents and dynamics gives way to the synergy which produces uniting symbols. What was previously our "work on the unconscious" here becomes "work with the unconscious" aimed at a true synthesis of the personality. The practice of active imagination corresponds to this aspect of our psychological endeavour.

While the distinction made above between the two phases of therapy is important, it should not be taken too literally. On closer examination, we see that right from the very onset of Jung's work, and from the very first meeting of our work with clients, the union of the opposites, far from emerging unexpectedly, is at the very centre of our attention. This can be seen in the constant attention which is directed towards the images presented in dreams and in the way we work on this material as an indication of one's psychic orientation. As far as Jung's comment regarding the absence of a specific method of his, useful in the analytical phase, we need to recognize that we have no psychological model which allows for the "analytical reduction" of complex psychic phenomena. We have nothing comparable to the biological model proposed by Freud nor to the social model espoused by Adler. From this point of view, it is undeniable that Jung has no specific methodological contribution to make to the analytical-reductive phase. And yet there is an original element of the Jungian approach which immediately, from the very start, is recognizable: the intense rapport which is established and maintained with the images produced by the psyche. One example of this is found, of course, in our work on dreams. Aside from the help these images provide for the understanding of psychic phenomena, our continued reflection on dream images creates, both cognitively and affectively, a connection and sense of togetherness between and among the various parts of the personality. Conscious and unconscious elements begin to dialogue between themselves as hypotheses of sense and meaning gradually emerge. This feeling of "togetherness" is an important counterweight to the sensations of fragmentation which so often accompany psychological disturbances. The sort of "familiarity" that emerges between conscious and unconscious contents gradually morphs into a basic trust in life itself, a most precious therapeutic factor.

We could say then that the Jungian approach, right from the very beginning, has an effect on the deeper part of the personality. This is and will continue to be the base on which a further synthesis of personality can be built. Psychological creativity does not suddenly spring up out of nowhere; it is rather like an underground river that waits for the right moment and the best conditions that will allow it to come to the surface.

The Inferior Dimension of the Psyche and the Process of Individuation

In order to gain our footing as we begin speaking about the imagination, let us once again take a look at the outline of Jungian typology and, taking for granted the reader's familiarity with the various terms of this diagram, turn our attention to the connection between them and the two phases of psychological work described by Jung.

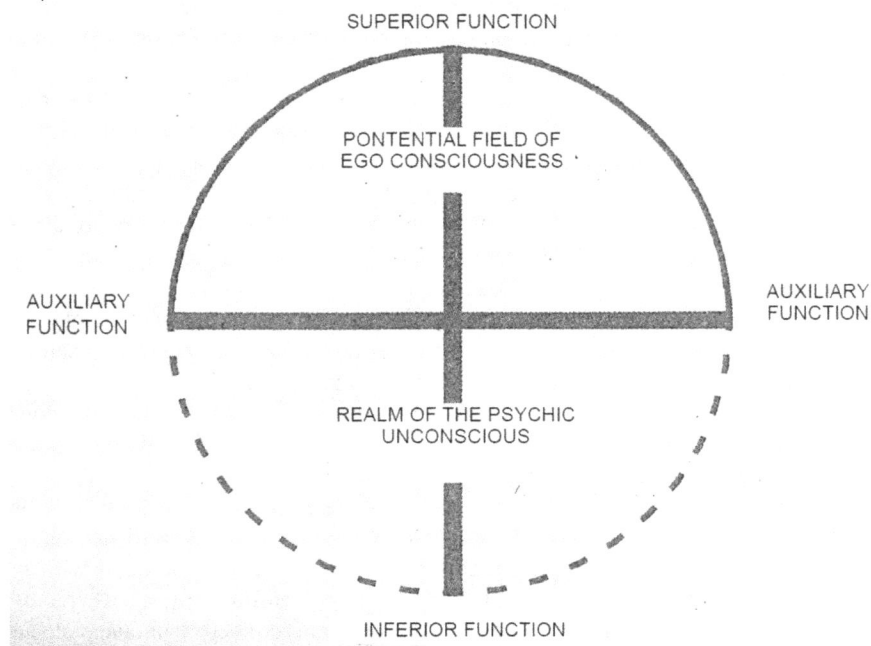

Figure 7

This classic representation of the functions (*thinking, feeling, sensation, intuition*) along the circumference of a circle in which two perpendicular lines have been drawn produces an upper semicircle, containing what is accessible to consciousness, and a lower one which is predominately the unconscious. At the top of the vertical line, we find the "superior function" which ego consciousness utilizes as its principal instrument of adaptation. At the two extremities of the horizontal line are the "auxiliary functions" which serve as an aid to conscious adaptation even though they, being situated on the dividing line between consciousness and the unconscious, are conditioned by the latter. These functions help in relativizing both the one-sidedness of the superior function and the identification ego consciousness establishes with it. The fluctuation of the dividing line between consciousness and the unconscious plays an important role in the contact which is made between the opposites. In the lower half of the circle, at the bottom of the vertical dividing line, we find the "inferior function" which corresponds to the unconscious root of the personality and the cardinal point for the whole question of active imagination. The perspective opened up for us by Jung has to do with the collective unconscious, and this permanent root in the world of the unconscious will necessarily be of the utmost importance for us.

The upper half of the circle used in our diagram depicts what happens as the conscious personality takes shape; clinically our work here entails the differentiation of conscious elements and the integration of those unconscious elements that exert undue pressure on consciousness. This is the area that psychoanalysis has traditionally been interested in. It is the seat of complex dynamics with rich overtones that will be helpful in the further development of the client, but virtually no attention is devoted to the lower part of the circle.

Let us imagine now that the therapeutic treatment has worked well. What will now become of the lower half of the diagram? What happens now to that irreducible reality of the unconscious where we ultimately have our roots? Will it be possible to maintain some sort of relationship with it? And if so, how? Our Jungian perspective opens up onto a vision of the unconscious that takes us beyond the confines of what is personal. Take for example the shadow side of the personality: on the one hand it can be explained and dealt with on the basis of the personal history of one's relationships and the ups and downs of the way we have adapted to life in general. Here we are in the realm of the personal unconscious which can be understood from a causal point of view. But from another point of view, we cannot overlook the collective determinants of the unconscious which shape the consciousness of individuals and of groups at large and which, in light of their absolute autonomy, cannot be subjected to a simple rational explanation.

The inferior dimension of the psyche contains the entire world of these aspects but, whereas the world of personal complexes can be explained and treated using analytical methods, the archetypal reality of the psyche cannot be dealt with in this way. What, from a personal point of view, can be confronted as a bothersome complex and so treated, is, from the perspective of the collective unconscious, a completely different question. Here we find the profoundly determining factors of our existence, those things which are no longer problems to be solved but realities we are called to live. Life brings us face to face with no end of problems, but life itself is not a problem we can find a solution to. It makes far more sense to see it as a mystery that needs to be recognized and honoured.

If we take this as our point of view, then the relationship we manage to establish with the inferior function becomes the special territory of the individuation process. Analysis will have created the basis by fostering, on the part of consciousness, a psychological sensitivity and attitude, but the final fruits of the process can be gained only by symbolic unification of the results of the work done so far with the unconscious. The goal of expanding the realm of the conscious at the cost of missing a chance to live the unconscious with greater spontaneity is an empty one, as if we were trying to empty the sea with the proverbial teaspoon. Consciousness is without a doubt the most precious human characteristic developed through the process of evolution and yet it would be wrong to consider it a goal in itself, instead of seeing it as a means we can use to touch another reality: the authenticity and fullness of existence.

The only way to really follow the path of individuation is to do it in harmony with the archetypal influences of the inferior side of the personality. Here we realize that far from being elements that can be brought under the control of consciousness, these unconscious dynamics are beyond our control and are not defects but rather reminders of the extent to which we belong to the unconscious, as nature herself ordained. Here we can discover that those parts of us which are impervious to proper adaptation often contain surprising and unexpected creative possibilities just as the "village idiot" found in so many fairytales is able to see what others miss and often is the only one capable of discovering the solution to difficult situations.

As Jung himself often said, the inferior function is the door that the angels and the devils of our existence use to enter our personalities; all of those things that arouse in us fear and a sense of wonder and which bypass the perception of the ordinary, everyday facts of life gain access through this special door. Symbolic contact with these manifestations of the archetypal aspects of life can give us a sense of the fullness of our existence. Without this opening onto the archetypal dimension of things we are destined to continually live with a deep sense of incompleteness and this in turn leads the ego to oscillate between feelings of omnipotence and impotence. Working on our relationship with the inferior function, from this point of view, can be seen as a watershed in the psychological *opus* of individuation.

Dreaming the Dream On

Active imagination is the practice indicated by Jung for those who want to follow the path of individuation as outlined above. The cornerstone of our encounters with the figures that people the unconscious is naturally the work we do on and with dreams; active imagination represents the development of this. Jung speaks about "dreaming the dream on" and makes references to a sort of dreaming with our eyes wide open. The interpretation of dream images is a kind of long-distance relationship between consciousness and the unconscious: during the dream state, the ego is absent and when the awake and attentive ego reflects on the dream, the dream itself is a mere memory. Active imagination allows space for a dialogue up close where ego consciousness and the figures of the unconsciousness interact on a new and different level which is neither completely conscious nor totally unconscious. The entire personality is involved in an intense experience of togetherness and while this can arouse powerful feeling reactions, the experience is not goal oriented but is important *just as it is*. Naturally one can find here any number of stimuli that involve thinking, feeling, sensation and intuition but this is an indirect effect. In a more direct sense, the only thing that really counts is that this meeting takes place. And in this way the personality experiences the unification of the very parts of itself. It is important not to idealize the experience as an ecstatic re-entry into Paradise; at times it arouses feelings of anguish and fear. What counts in the end is this contact with and among the parts of us and the new synergy that is created and which replaces the profound sensation of dissociation that plagues ego consciousness. It is clear from Jung's pronouncements that active imagination was, for him, the best way to pave the way for the operation of the transcendent function, that part of the psyche's work which allows for the opposition between internal factors to be bridged in a symbolic way and to further develop.

After these considerations related to the theoretical underpinnings of the practice, we now need to examine the "nuts and bolts" of how to proceed. We naturally will not be able to deal with all the variables that comprise such a complex topic and, as said earlier, the best way to hand on the important elements of the procedure is through personal, word of mouth communication. Nonetheless, some observations as to how to proceed are in order.

Generally speaking, the best way to begin is by being accompanied by one's analyst with whom so much work will have been done on the symbolic interpretation of dreams and symptoms. Unfortunately, not all analysts with a Jungian formation are really familiar with the use of active imagination; in these cases, it is advisable to consult an analyst who has experience in this field. It is most important that especially in the early phases of this work there be a space for exchange with an experienced analyst in order to avoid feelings of isolation. The person chosen to listen to the active imagination experienced by a patient must do so without intervening or interfering in the individual process in any way. If necessary, limited comments on the methodology used by the patient can be interjected.

It is important to note that the imaginative process is to be carried forward in solitude, something Jung was clear about. The imaginal setting in by its very nature internal and is entrusted exclusively to the personal responsibility of the individual. While engaging in the process, the presence of others, including the analyst, is not allowed, otherwise the deepest meaning of the experience – the symbolic synthesis of one's own personality – will be interfered with. In psychological terms, who we really are, in the final analysis, is a deep personal mystery.

Ethical Confrontation with the Unconscious

In practical terms, the procedure of active imagination follows a series of fundamental steps. Marie-Louise von Franz has aptly outlined four of them: first, it is important to create a void and to empty the mind of our ordinary state of consciousness, second, one needs to clearly "establish the image" from which the procedure will proceed, maintaining a level of concentration that will allow for the activation of the image (*let things happen*). Third, it is important to "objectify" the encounter, documenting it through writing, drawing etc. Finally, one needs to take seriously the ethical encounter with the unconscious, that is interact with the unconscious images in such a way as to have a say in the outcome of the encounter.

The first three steps outlined above correspond to the way most forms of medi-tation proceed while the fourth, the ethical encounter with the encounter, defines active imagination as a specifically psychological form of meditation. What Jung called the "ethical confrontation" is central to the whole endeavour: when the pro-cedure reaches its peak, the opposing psychic levels of consciousness and the un-conscious will dialogue and interact with one another within a framework that concerns both of them and contributes to a mutual solution.

This passage is of the highest significance because it expresses the activation of a true symbolic form of consciousness. Through this procedure, a form of ethical maturity which goes well beyond the ideological or normative paradigm collec-tively held as valid, is reached. This path is by no means simple; it requires symbolic delicacy but also discipline. We need only think of the labours of Jung, carried out in total solitude, as he worked on his *Red Book*. The psychological-ethical stance of the personality takes shape thanks to this direct dialogue between its component parts, helping us avoid that tendency towards splitting, to which ego consciousness is so prone. This is the moment in which the opposites meet to create a form of synergy, and this is, in essence, the goal and meaning of active imagination. The ego is not asked to step out of the picture; the expressions "dreaming with eyes wide open" and "dreaming the dream on" express very aptly the fact that consciousness is pre-sent and "active" during the procedure. Instead of stepping out of the picture, what consciousness needs to do is to recognize that the images arising from the uncon-scious are an "active" part of the search for truth, with all that this mutual participa-tion implies in terms of one's ethical position. The ego – our necessary functional complex as far as the management of life and the interpretation of phenomena are concerned – will continue to express its needs and formulate its hypotheses but at the same time all of its efforts need to be brought into line with the point of view of the unconscious; both parties have equal dignity and will have a voice in the process.

As this dialogue between the parts of ourselves starts to occupy more space at the centre of the personality, we also need to recognize just how complex we are and allow ourselves to function for what we are. If we keep on believing in a form of undifferentiated unity in the personality, then we are bound to slip into an indi-vidual and collective form of splitting. Dr Jekyll's admirable search for the elixir of a long life will, sooner or later, have to take into serious consideration what his dark brother, Mr Hyde, has to say about the matter!

The Inner Feeling of Community

There are a great many aspects of the procedure of active imagination that we could examine, but here it would be a good idea to have a look at the special relationship that can take shape between ourselves and some important figures that emerge within the imaginal scene. It often happens that a psychic image takes on special weight and meaning, appearing often or in various circumstances within one's imaginative journey. Occurrences such as these (which are by no means rare) offer an opportunity to establish a special interior rapport which can be an important point of reference as time goes on.

As a general rule, it is advisable to allow the imaginal scene lived in these experiences to develop over time in a continuous way so that the questions or problems that have been posed can be dealt with in depth, rather than jumping from one of the many images the richness of the unconscious proposes, to another and then to another. The "active" role of consciousness also consists in resisting the attraction and fascination of the varied images that pop up along the way, with the passivity that allows the flow of images to sweep away the ego. Just as we need to regularly frequent the important people in our outer lives such as close friends and those we have deep sentimental relations with, so in the inner world must we allow our rapport with imaginal figures to deepen through regularity. Figures of this nature take on a depth and importance that become a vital part of our psychic life. In this way we can actually encourage the unconscious to manifest itself in personifications which in turn become our partners in dialogue. All of this gives body and substance to the ethical maturity mentioned above.

The sense of community and of social contact that we live in our concrete lives becomes present within us, in the inner world, as we cultivate dialogue and exchanges with the figures of the psyche. This produces a counterweight to the one-sidedness of the ego which tends to assume on its own the management of life in general; a more active participation on the part of the unconscious makes the choices of our existence, whether they be of consequence or not, more significant and complete.

The more we become familiar with the internal dialogue that helps develop a rapport with the characters that populate the world of the unconscious, the more we will be able to limit both the emotional overload and the exaggerated projections which often accompany our relationships in the concrete world. Many personal, social and political questions along with issues of general public interest could be dealt with better if the voice of the unconscious were listened to and heeded. We should avoid thinking and acting as if paying attention to "the voices within" were an exclusively psychotic phenomenon; this attitude, in the end, can be seen as one of the shadows of the catastrophic state the ego is in. The ego's hypertrophic state drowns out the polyphony of the psyche whose diversity is so great that when unduly compressed, it explodes in critical events of both a personal and a collective nature. The spiritual and psychological advantages of active imagination can be a precious resource in preparing for catastrophic happenings and help create in the individual a readiness to live the symbolic reality of the diversity each of us carries within, with an openness that allows us to leave space for the diversity and to take it seriously. Jung himself compared the act of "dreaming the dream on" through active imagination to an "anticipated psychosis"; what he means by this is that the rupture of a psychosis is avoided because the diversity is accepted and supported by consciousness. An approach of this type better prepares us to face the events and challenges of outer life as well, because we will have become familiar with the "choral" reality of our own inner lives, more familiar and cautious regarding the thirst for control which the ego so often displays, and wary of its obsessive tendency and its penchant for violently projecting its own shadow onto the reality of others. In short, the imaginative work of individuation is not limited to the way we treat and interact with our inner lives, and it would be indeed misleading to conclude this. This practice helps us to better live our relationships in the outer world since it aids in becoming deeply rooted in a profound sense of symbolic participation.

Another important aspect of active imagination is the way it helps in the work of dream interpretation, allowing for a lively dialogue with inner figures about the questions presented by the dream material. Naturally, it is important to avoid generalizing, and yet this approach can be particularly helpful when the impact of inner figures on the ego is especially potent creating the need to establish the right distance between these two elements. In these cases, the help of an inner figure within whom the dreamer has developed a relationship can be of great value, most notably when the dream contains a numinous element that might overly tax or inflate the ego. Dialogue with a familiar inner figure whose point of view may be different from the ego's can be very valuable, This is comparable to what happens with the analyst when we feel we are tied in knots, trying to work through a difficult dream message. Thanks to active imagination, one's own inner figures can have this role and make up for subjective shortcomings in the ego's point of view. This interplay between active imagination and dream work is important, as already noted, with regards to the delicate question of "dissolving the transference" as it allows for the transition from the *analytical setting* to the *imaginal setting*.

There are many other elements and aspects of active imagination that could be mentioned and that might help in understanding the real fruits of the practice, but time and space make it necessary to limit our exposition here. What is important to keep in mind is that imaginative processes play a particularly important role in the *opus* of uniting the opposites. Individuals who have experienced the work of symbolically interpreting dreams will feel prepared to face this task, overcoming the obstacles of resistance, of the concretistic attitude of our culture, of the need to constantly make reference to scientific paradigms, and of a sort of inflation of the *Persona* which would prefer to feel safe and sound within the certainties of professional procedure. It is indeed serious that this approach is continually neglected from analytical training.

Despite the obstacles and difficulties that one may encounter, what really matters is the honesty with which one approaches this practice. It is the only way to truly respect and participate in the legacy of Jung. The path of individuation leads us here.

Chapter 4

Is Active Imagination the Sleeping Beauty of Analytical Psychology?

Gaetana Bonasera
Translated by Alessia Marzano

Introduction

It is my intention, in this chapter, to address the topic of Active Imagination starting from the results of the research carried out by Dr. Chiara Tozzi (Tozzi, 2023) with the support of the International Association for Analytical Psychology (IAAP), which investigated, through a questionnaire addressed to trainees, training analysts, and routers around the world, knowledge about Active Imagination, its employment in training courses, in personal analysis and clinical practice. The data that emerged from the research emphasizes that, while recognizing the centrality and importance of Active Imagination for Jung, this practice is underused today, both in research and training, compared with other tools (Tozzi, 2023). What is happening? Has Active Imagination become the Cinderella, if not the Sleeping Beauty of analytical psychology?

Before analyzing the possible reasons behind the data that emerged from the research, I consider it necessary, if not indispensable, to start with the protagonist of our understanding: Active Imagination.

What Is Active Imagination?

When Carl Gustav Jung's *The Red Book: Liber Novus* was first published in 2009 (2010 in Italy), it was clear to all that the book, which had aroused so much curiosity and mystery, was an "exercise" in Active Imagination, a practice that Jung used as a tool for investigation and analysis of the unconscious. Through his own experience, and later that of his patients, Jung perfected a meditation-like tool in a lifelong journey where the ego voluntarily comes into contact and dialogue with images surfacing from the unconscious. The refinement of this tool occurred during Jung's work on himself from 1912 to 1917 when he went through a deep inner crisis following his rupture with Freud. *The Red Book* is structured as a diary recording Jung's intense and suffering experience. Active Imagination became his preferred method to get in touch with the images of the unconscious. Jung called this practice "Active Imagination" to distinguish it from passive imagination, a spontaneous activity of the psyche, with no intervention of the ego, which functions

DOI: 10.4324/9781003411369-4

only as a spectator. Active Imagination also differs from fantasizing; in this case, the ego uses imagination to escape reality. In Active Imagination, the ego interacts with personifications of the parts of the unconscious without "manipulating" them by letting them manifest, "letting be. . ." Active Imagination, which Jung called, *cum grano salis*, an *anticipated psychosis*, differs from such forms of fantasizing in that the individual wholly and consciously enters the event (von Franz, 2002 in De Luca Comandini & Mercurio, 2002, p. 258).

For Jung, the image is the native language of the unconscious, *die Große Sprache*, as Michael Ende expressed in his *Neverending Story*. Already in his childhood,[1] Jung had the intuition that we are not alone, that an underground and mysterious world inhabits us, seeking to make contact with us. Then, during the years of the "great crisis," Jung experienced that the unconscious lives a life parallel to our daily conscious existence. A life that we can grasp at night through dream activity and during the day when the threshold of consciousness is lowered, through glimpses that open up like breaches – only to see them immediately fade – as fragments of the film of our inner life that, like a river, flows uninterrupted.

In conscious reality, a single identity represents us through the narrative of our lives, from birth to death, passing through the events that happen to us. In the unconscious, identities can be multiple; thousands of images can represent every part and every aspect of our person. These two realms live, interact, and influence each other. Entering this dimension is like visiting an unfamiliar planet. Like all unfamiliar places, it hides pitfalls; Jung himself warned of the dangers of engaging in such activity.

In *The Red Book*, Jung describes this experience as descending into absolute obscurity, and the experience of being confronted with the images of our Shadow can be a terrifying experience, which might remind us of Dante's journey into hell; however, unlike the latter, the prerequisite for exercising it is to go into it without a guide. Entering the underworld is the journey of the search for the Self. Some keep away from it, or, if they try to enter, flee immediately in terror; some enter and are so fascinated by it that they never want to go back; there are those who, on the other hand, get lost and can no longer find their way back; and finally those who, after traveling and exploring it, facing monsters, demons, dark and mysterious entities, return transformed. If our conscious life is one-sided – as we always choose sides, one way or another – dualism reigns in the subterranean life; everything has its opposite so that if one thing is true, the opposite is also true. Here we can find everything and nothing, good and evil, day and night, good and bad, sweetness and harshness, goodness and brutality, wonder and horror, love and hate, reason and delusion, and life and death.

Through Active Imagination, it is possible to enter this subterranean dimension. As Jung claims, from the contrast between the divergent positions of the ego and the unconscious, we can create unifying symbols that contain and transcend the opposing positions giving rise to new possibilities and allowing the process of *individuation*.

How to Proceed on the Path to Active Imagination

First, I consider it essential to clarify why, for Jung, Active Imagination is the pivot of analytic psychology. According to Jung, the automatic production of unconscious fantasies, their succession, and confrontation with them lead to the gradual transformation of autonomous complexes.

> This transformation is the aim of the analysis of the unconscious. If there is no transformation, it means that the determining influence of the unconscious is unabated, and that it will in some cases persist in maintaining neurotic symptoms in spite of all our analysis and all our understanding. Alternatively, a compulsive transference will take hold, which is just as bad as a neurosis.
>
> (Jung, 1972, p. 291)

Active Imagination is an experience that takes place in the inner world instead of in the external world. Jung never made sharp distinctions between what is real and non-real; for him, "real" is that which acts, bringing transformation (1972, p. 297). In the world of the ego, we are used to thinking that the external world is the real one, while the inner world is populated only by fantasies as if the "real" were a prerogative of matter. However, we know that the psyche, the inner world, is just as real; it is living matter.

Neuroscience has recently confirmed that the brain does not distinguish between images from the outside world and those from the inner world (Kosslyn et al., 2001). For centuries we have been conditioned to separate inside and outside, mind and body, attributing the origin of the real only to the external world. It is with these conditionings that we approach Active Imagination.

To facilitate the understanding and implementation of the procedure, von Franz (1980) proposes following four different stages, which, among other things, characterize and differentiate the work of Active Imagination from other similar "techniques". The necessary precondition is the absence of the analyst. The latter must never assist or intervene in the process; their presence will unfold through respectful and nonjudgmental listening. Let us take a closer look at these stages:

1   To begin this experience, creating an external and internal vacuum is necessary so that the ego's thought processes slumber and suspend its critical activity. Creating a psychic vacuum allows us to open a space for "letting things happen"; thus, it is necessary to enter a state of relaxation that allows the threshold of consciousness to approach that of the unconscious. For this purpose, being in a quiet environment and fully self-aware is critical. In contrast to a simple meditative state, an Active Imagination may begin with an image or emotion that forcefully presents itself to the ego's attention, demanding consideration. Jung advises taking one's affective condition as a starting point and focusing on the state of mind one is in by sinking into it without prejudice.

2   It is then possible to focus on the image that emerges, maintaining an attitude of openness and acceptance. At this stage, von Franz suggests avoiding two kinds of mistakes: fixating too much on an image, blocking it out by immediately looking for its meaning, and avoiding the personifications of the unconscious changing abruptly as in a kind of internal film. Instead, attention should be held long enough to get in touch with the image and ask questions. In Active Imagination, the role of the ego is essential; it should not be passive but active toward the emerging personifications of the unconscious. In his essay "The Transcendent Function," Jung warns us about the mind's deceptions: constant intrusions of the consciousness that judge and devalue all images that arise. Jung himself fought against his own mockery, disdain for the activity of fantasizing, and rational doubts. Besides, the ego may linger on aesthetic processing, trying to "correct" the image as if it were a kind of work of art and, in an attempt to master its form, neglecting the message the image is seeking to convey (von Franz, 1980).

3   In the third stage, supporting the unconscious with a creative form of expression is vital; this can be indifferently writing, painting, sculpture, dance, or music according to one's inclination and feeling or, as Jung would say, according to one's psychological type. However, as de Luca Comandini (2002) suggests, whatever form it takes, a hint of verbalization can still be helpful, recalling that, in *Mysterium Coniunctionis*, Jung himself, describing the method of Active Imagination, evokes the formal unavoidability of language, indispensable to fix the actual reality of things (de Luca Comandini, 2002, p. 145).

Nonetheless, we cannot speak of true Active Imagination without considering the fourth stage.

4   Through Active Imagination, the ego and the unconscious may initiate an "ethical confrontation". The ego must dialogue on an equal footing with the images of the unconscious. This passage involves taking the messages from our deepest part seriously while maintaining the same ethical attitude as if listening to another person of equal rank and dignity.

Returning to what we have called *Phase* 1, according to which it is necessary to seclude oneself and create a mental vacuum, the first difficulties arise. First, it proves challenging to think that what one is about to experience is real. Besides, the ego sets up a series of defenses:

•   Difficulty in letting go and maintaining an empty mind; the ego, accustomed to controlling, surrenders with incredible difficulty. To this end, it constantly attempts to take control of the images and the experience.

•   According to von Franz's and Jung's reports, in an accurate Active Imagination, the ego should go through everything that happens without escaping. However, if this happens, that is, if the ego tries to rewind the "film" and find a different ending, the patient is considered to be "cheating".

• We also cannot fail to consider the unconscious defenses that try to prevent one from confronting images that have been protected and preserved (dissociated) to avoid suffering and pain.

To describe the difficulties in which the ego finds itself when faced with the experience of Active Imagination, the words of Elizabeth Lloyd Mayer (2007) appear as particularly appropriate:

> We have to give up one thing in order to see the other. We have to lose what's familiar in order to see what's new. Some losses are easy, like giving up a chalice to see profiles. But some losses aren't easy at all. Giving up our habitual grounding in rational thought to see something else, even just for a moment, that's anything but easy for most of us.
>
> (p. 137)

When the images finally begin to flow, and suddenly one finds oneself inside the imagination, the feeling is as strange as if there were a change of register. It is a matter of coming out of the seriousness of the ego, of breaking the patterns. To describe what happens with visuals, I am reminded of two scenes: the first is from the famous movie *Mary Poppins* (1964), in which Mary and Bert (the chimney sweep) enter the drawings that come alive and interact with them. The second one is from the book *The Neverending Story* (Ende, 1984), in which the protagonist Bastian Balthazar Bux finds himself part of the story he reads and interacts with the characters. It is about learning to "hallucinate" under the control of the ego, which must be able to take an intermediate position between "letting happen" and "controlling" the experience.

Why Is Active Imagination Scary?

As we have seen from the results of Tozzi's research (2023), there is evidence of some difficulty on the part of many colleagues in accepting and using a method that favors working with the image and the imagination, the cornerstones of analytic psychology, as Jung conceived it. Active Imagination, then, despite its importance within analytic psychology, seems to be falling into disuse, both in research and training. A slightly countervailing finding seems to be the use of Active Imagination in clinical practice compared with its teaching in training courses and research.

I realize that even from the description of the stages of Active Imagination, one can sense the difficulty of putting it into practice. It may even seem like a fool's errand, the beginning of true derangement. Previously I mentioned "learning to hallucinate" or "anticipated psychosis" as Jung puts it in *Mysterium coniunctionis*

(1970); these statements are undoubtedly frightening, invoking the specter of psychosis. Jung states that Active Imagination could create latent psychosis (von Franz, 2002, in De Luca Comandini & Mercurio, 2002, p. 261). Therefore, von Franz affirms that "active imagination is a dangerous tool that should not be practiced without expert assistance" (De Luca Comandini & Mercurio, 2002, p. 260). Could these warnings have caused an overly cautious attitude and discouraged its use? However, for Jung, even the analysis may prove dangerous for strongly dissociated persons at risk of psychosis.

Active Imagination and all of Jung's work has always been shrouded in an aura of mistrust and prejudice. In her book *C.G. Jung, His Myth in Our Time* (1998), von Franz narrates that

> his loyalty to the relation to the inner "genius" or "daemon," as one might also call it provoked mistrust and aversion in many people, almost as if he himself appeared to them as that daemon of the unconscious of which they were so afraid. This still seems to me to be the case, more or less, even today. The name of Jung seldom leaves people cold; one almost always comes up against emotionally charged rejection or enthusiasm whenever one mentions him [. . .] On closer examination, however, these reactions are generally directed at that god or demon, the unconscious, whose existence many modern people do not wish to recognize, [. . .] without noticing that they are motivated by fear. Jung's work is therefore conspicuous as a stumbling block in the contemporary intellectual scene. It is too fundamental, in a sense, to be modern.
>
> (p. 62)

Nonetheless, let us leave behind the prejudices about Jung and return to the difficulties of practicing Active Imagination. Even the mere thought of predisposing the ego to abandon strict control over reality can generate anxiety, discouraging its use. Elie Humbert (1978) tells us that "such readiness presupposes a softening of defense mechanisms and a certain freedom in relation to the need to imitate" (p. 91).

For this reason, Active Imagination can presumably be exercised more toward the end of the analysis when the individuation process is already underway and the patient's personality is more evolved. Furthermore, it is crucial to consider the difficulty of the ego to escape the overload of stimuli to which we are continually subjected, which leads us to experience a kind of *horror vacui*. In our society, which primarily values looking outward, turning the gaze toward the Self is considered an activity that excludes the outside world. De Luca Comandini (2002, p. 24) warns us against falling into the error typical of Western culture, of misunderstanding the terms introvert and extrovert. While in many other cultures, self-awareness is the foundation of social relations, in the West, the inner experience is viewed with suspicion and devalued because it is understood as disconnected from the real. For analytical psychology, inner experiences give prominence and consistency to personal authenticity and express a precious social value (De Luca Comandini,

2002, p. 25). Reaching out to the darkest parts of the personality allows for genuine contact with the Other by neutralizing projections underlying prejudice, hatred, and war. The Shadow plays a central role in the vision and knowledge of reality and the Other.

The parts we refuse to see and accept that we allow to slip into the unconscious become a matter that can be projected outward, conditioning the vision of – an encounter with – the Other, who becomes the unconscious receptacle of our rejected parts.

The work on light and Shadow, oriented toward the integration of the opposites, consciousness, and the unconscious, is both intrapsychic – aimed at the recovery of the removed dark parts and the archetypal parts rooted in the ancient social world – and intersubjective, focusing on the relationship with the Other, stripped of the projections. Therefore, the encounter with the Other-from-self is primarily the encounter with the Other-in-self and presupposes a work of knowing one's own Shadow and a withdrawal of projections as fragmented parts. Cultivating imaginative intelligence, therefore, fosters the development of an inner balance that helps experience external reality, something that is particularly difficult today more than in the past.

Furthermore, pursuing possible causes of the limited use of Active Imagination, we can also count, from my perspective, the demonization that fantastic imagination has suffered for several centuries at the hands of the Catholic Church – e.g., the witch-hunt – as it was considered the source of evil and subsequently of psychic evil. In his book, *The Relations between the Ego and the Unconscious* (1972, p. 136), Jung blames the scientific creed of our time for developing and nurturing a superstitious phobia toward fantastic imagination. Even today, fantastic imagination is despised, devalued, and relegated to a mere playful product resulting from emotional states, as opposed to the supremacy of logic and reason. The result is penalization and near exclusion of depth psychology, particularly analytical psychology, in universities, in contrast with cognitive-behavioral psychology teachings. Above all, analytical psychology, anchored in the subjective feelings of those who carry it out, does not qualify for objective and empirical verifications that can be measured quantitatively, according to the canons of the scientific method (De Luca Comandini, 2002). Notably, Active Imagination, taking place in the inner world, offers no observable and measurable support.

Such practice can be seen as a feared weapon, kept at a distance, evoking evil, death, and destruction. Contact with the unconscious and our dark parts continues to be a *taboo*, pushing us to anchor ourselves in the rational, more easily observed, and controlled part. One of the possible ways to delve into the unconscious is through the symbolism of dreams, whose mediation is entrusted not only to the ego but also to the reassuring figure of the analyst. Unlike the dream, a spontaneous product of the unconscious, Active Imagination fosters the "transcendent function," that is, the function that sets in motion the synthesis of the conscious and unconscious personality, inducing a more rapid and profound maturation (von Franz, 2002, in De Luca Comandini & Mercurio, 2002).

"No one who strives for selfhood (individuation) is spared this dangerous passage . . . a dangerous reversal of the aims and intentions of the conscious mind. It is a sacrifice of the ego's stability and a surrender to the extreme uncertainty of what must seem like a chaotic riot of phantasmal forms" (Jung, 1991, p. 327). In such a process, the ego with its certainties is no longer the protagonist; the process naturally "occurs" (Aversa, 2013, p. 32). In this regard, Luigi Aversa writes:

> In occurrence there is the unpersonal dimension that marks the crisis of all guarantees. [. . .] In order for something to occur, one must reach, contact a limit that we can perceive only in the terms that Karl Jaspers would call "cipher". The "cipher" is what marks the impossibility of each certainty and opens up to the further sense t; at is symbolic experience; like the symbol, the "cipher" "breaks up" the fixed meanings in favour of an as yet unknown dimension which in its "opening up" constantly requires new meanings.
>
> (1987, p. 42, in Aversa, 2013, p. 32)

Another reason for the decline of Active Imagination can be traced, at least in Italy, to the race for the recognition of schools of specialization in psychotherapy within academic and health institutions. This achievement led to leveling the specificities of the different orientations, particularly for depth psychology (De Luca Comandini, 2002, p. 29). After the penalization suffered in academia for deviating from the positive science model, the need for visibility and redemption has led the associations, which for years carried forward Jungian thought, to a gradual loss of their specificity, of their "individuation," pushing strongly toward a homologation that goes, in fact, against the cardinal principles of analytical psychology itself.

Ethics and Active Imagination

Here we come to one of the central and most important aspects of Active Imagination and one of my main interests. Ethical responsibility occupies an innovative, decisive role in Jung's work (Humbert, 1978, p. 95). Ethics runs through and permeates the whole Jungian thought and affects, albeit in different ways, the individual in general, society, and those involved in the analytic process. The final objective of self-development, and thus of the individuation process, places the individual with an *ethical ego* at the center, that is, one capable of facing and integrating all parts of his or her personality, whether conscious or unconscious. Jung considers the individuation process an ethical duty of the human being to his or her soul, which continually aims to achieve its ultimate goal: self-realization and self-completion. Thus, individuation is, for Jung, a spontaneous process of growth and maturation inscribed in being: "I use the term 'individuation' to denote the process by which a person becomes a psychological 'in-dividual,' that is, a separate, indivisible unity or 'whole'" (Jung, 1980, p. 275, par. 490). The self bears within itself the character of realization, and loss and inauthenticity are witnessed as bringing discomfort, suffering, and pathology. For Jung, the "betrayal" of the predisposition to Self-realization leads the individual toward a state of inauthentic existence. This betrayal is expressed by the denial of the unconscious and the misrecognition of the process of individuation.

With Jung, ethics enters the analytic setting, bringing a radical change. The classic image of the analyst sitting behind the couch claiming neutrality, one of the most important rules of the analytic setting, so dear to Freud, lapses. According to Jung (1933):

> the relation between physician and patient remains personal within the frame of the impersonal, professional treatment. We cannot by any device bring it about that the treatment is not the outcome of a mutual influence in which the whole being of the patient as well as that of the doctor plays its part [. . .] For this reason the personalities of the doctor and patient have often more to do with the outcome of the treatment than what the doctor says or thinks – although we must not undervalue this latter factor as a disturbing or healing one. The meeting of two personalities is like the contact of two chemical substances: if there is any reaction, both are transformed. We should expect the doctor to have an influence on the patient in every effective psychic treatment; but this influence can only take place when he too is affected by the patient. You can exert no influence if you are not susceptible to influence. It is futile for the doctor to shield himself from the influence of the patient and to surround himself with a smoke-screen of fatherly and professional authority. If he does so he merely forbids himself the use of a highly important organ of information, and the patient influences him unconsciously none the less. The unconscious changes in the doctor which the patient thus brings about are well known to many psychotherapists; they are disturbances, or even injuries, peculiar to the profession, which illustrate in a striking way the patient's almost "chemical" influence.
>
> (p. 49)

For Jung, the analyst's ethical attitude shifts the focus of the analysis to the relationship. Thus, the analyst is no longer a neutral observer of intrapsychic mechanisms but a subject who hits the field entering a relationship with the patient. The analyst is no longer just a professional caring for a sick person but an ethically conscious and responsible subject who respects the patient and the treatment process. Jung believes the most significant value of analytic psychology – and depth psychology in general – lies in consciousness's deepening. In this sense, becoming conscious is not so much a technical expedient as it is an ethical pursuit (Zoja, 2011, p. 27). Zoja (2011) states that by foregrounding the ethical attitude, the analyst increases the levels of complexity, including "not only the conscious norms of our actions and the goals to which we consciously aspire, but also our unconscious omissions and all the complex motivations that can overtake us in the course of an already well-intentioned act". We thus speak of ethics "that holds us accountable to intentional consequences, but also unintentional and unconscious ones" (p. 127).

The deepening of consciousness is the work to be pursued with the analysand, albeit being the analyst's primary responsibility, not only during personal analysis but continuously, with each patient and at each session. Consequently, the commitment of the analyst increases, as do the elements and levels that must be considered in the work to be done: the consciousness of the patient, the consciousness of the analyst, the unconscious of the patient, and the unconscious of the analyst, plus the relationships that occur between these parts. Besides, other levels provide a frame: the society in which we operate, its rules, and all the other major and minor systems to which the participants belong.

Analysts and patients hold a great responsibility in the ethical setting while occupying different positions. The analyst has the ethical duty to encourage and respect the images emerging from the patient's unconscious while promoting the patient's autonomy from the analysis. Additionally, the analyst has an ethical duty to bring themselves and their images into the field. On the other hand, the patient has an ethical duty toward the images emerging from their unconscious and an ethical duty toward their individuation, realization, and search for the Self.

As outlined by von Franz in step 4, regarding the practice of Active Imagination, this cannot be defined as such without the ethical confrontation with images. Therefore, as previously mentioned, the patient must confront the images that come from their unconscious and understand that everything happening to them does not happen to their image. Additionally, the patient must recognize the images as parts of themselves, not as objects of their imagination.

Having to carry out the experience of Active Imagination alone, without the analyst's presence, also fits into the ethical context of the analytic setting. For Jung, it is of paramount importance to bring the patient to be independent of the analysis and the analyst; he considers Active Imagination a "form of meditation as the criteria of whether an analysand was willing to take responsibility for himself or would seek to continue forever living as a parasite on his analyst" (von Franz, 2014, p. 123). Moreover, Jung considers this tool fundamental to resolving transference, the impasse at the end of analysis often attributed to the patient's own predicaments.

As Neumann (1990) writes,

> The principal requirement of the new ethic is not that the individual should be "good", but that he should be psychologically autonomous – that is to say, healthy and productive, and yet at the same time not psychologically infectious. And the autonomy of the ethical personality means essentially that the assimilation and use of the negative forces to be found in every psychic system takes place as far as possible consciously, within the process of self-realisation.
>
> (p. 102)

Nevertheless, how prepared and willing is the analyst to let go of the patient, and more importantly, how willing is he or she to give up the rewarding role of the healer?

The analytic relationship, in which the analyst plays the savior role and encourages dependence and power over the patient, activates a series of perverse dynamics. While on the one hand, the patient is de-empowered and cured, on the other hand, the gap between the two positions increases, with the analyst becoming increasingly influential on one side and the patient increasingly powerless on the other. In these cases, the analyst may well succeed in helping the patient to achieve stability or alleviate neurotic symptoms but not in embarking on a path of individuation since, as Jung says, the analyst cannot take his or her patients any farther than he or she has gone (Guggenbühl-Craig, 1990).

Moreover, from his position of inferiority, the patient tends to idealize the powerful analyst who is admired and revered; at the same time, idealization opens the door to envy, destructive impulses, and *negative transference*.

Conclusive Remarks

In light of what has been analyzed, the question arises as to whether Active Imagination, while a powerful and effective – albeit risky tool, may prove anti-beneficial and unconventional for the analyst.

As we have seen, Active Imagination is the most powerful tool for influencing the unconscious and fostering the patient's personal stability and autonomy. However, this can only happen if the patient is adequately supported by an analyst trained in such practice.

What future can Active Imagination have if analysts are unwilling to confront themselves and the patient ethically? What future can analytic psychology have if analysts and future analysts do not familiarize themselves with and experience the power of their inner images either during training or in their personal analysis?

Is the practice of Active Imagination bound to disappear from the scenario of analytical psychology?

Thankfully, the research results (Tozzi, 2023) revealed some reassuring data. Many participants expressed a genuine desire and willingness to learn more about Active Imagination. This data could be an essential clue, representing a "beginning" that, if grasped and embraced, could breathe new life into a practice so dear to Jung and awaken it from the lethargy into which it seems to have fallen.

Notes

1 See *Memories, Dreams, Reflections*, 1995.

References

Adorisio, A. *L'immaginazione attiva: origini ed evoluzione* [Active imagination: origins and evolution]. *Quaderni di cultura junghiana, Psiche: Rappresentazioni, Raffigurazioni, Configurazioni*, 2(2). Ed. Cipa, Rome [in Italian], 2013.

Aversa, L. *C.G. Jung: il senso psicologico dell'esistenza* [C.G. Jung: The Psychological Meaning of Experience]. In L. Aversa, M. Caci, A. Connolly, V.M. De Marinis, A. Gianni,

M. Giannoni, A. Iapoce, M.I. Marozza, E.V. Trapanese, *Riflettere con Jung* [Understanding Jung]. Fattore Umano Editore, 2013.

De Luca Comandini, F. Immaginazione attiva. Senso interno e valenze sociali dell'individualità psicologica [Active Imagination. Internal sense and social meanings of psychological individuality], in F. De Luca Comandini & R. Mercurio (eds.), *L'Immaginazione Attiva* [Active Imagination], La biblioteca di Vivarum, Milan, 2002.

De Luca Comandini, F., and R. Mercurio (eds.), *L'Immaginazione Attiva* [Active Imagination], La biblioteca di Vivarum, Milan, 2002.

Ende, M. *The Neverending Story*. Penguin Books, London, 1984.

Guggenbühl-Craig, A. *Power in the Helping Professions*. Spring Publications, 10th ed., 1990.

Humbert, E. *I tre verbi dell'immaginazione attiva* [The three verbs of Active Imagination]. *Rivista di psicologia analitica*, 17, Marsilio Editore [in Italian], 1978.

Jung, C.G. *Modern Man in Search of a Soul*, trans. W.S. Dell and C.F. Baynes, Harvest, 1933.

Jung, C.G. *Mysterium coniunctionis*, in *Collected Works of C.G. Jung, Vol. 14*. 2nd ed., Princeton University Press, 1970.

Jung, C.G. The Relations between the Ego and the Unconscious. Two Essays in Analytical Psychology. *The Collected Works of C.G. Jung*, Vol. 7, Bollingen Series XX, 2nd edn, trans. R.F.C. Hull, Princeton University Press, 1972.

Jung, C.G. *The Archetypes and the Collective Unconscious*, Vol. 9i, Bollingen Paperback printing, Princeton University Press, 1980.

Jung, C.G., and Hull, R.F.C. Psychological Commentary on the Tibetan Book of the Dead, in Violet S. de Laszlo (ed.), *Psyche and Symbol: A Selection from the Writings of C.G. Jung* (pp. 313–332), Vol. 661. Princeton University Press, 1991. doi:10.2307/j.ctv19fvxpz

Jung, C.G., and Jaffè, A. (ed.). *Memories, Dreams, Reflections* [Erinnerungen, Träume, Gedanken], Fontana Press, 1995.

Jung, C.G. *The Red Book: Liber Novus* (S. Shamdasani, Ed.; M. Kyburz, J. Peck, & S. Shamdasani, trans.). W.W. Norton & Company, 2009.

Kosslyn, S.M., Ganis, G., and Thompson, W.L. Mental imagery: Neural representations and psychological dimensions. *Nature Reviews Neuroscience*, 2(10), 635–642, 2001. doi:10.1038/35090055

Lloyd Mayer, E. *Extraordinary Knowing: Science, Skepticism, and the Inexplicable Powers of the Human Mind*. Bantam Dell Publishing Group, 2007.

Neumann, E. (1990). *Depth Psychology and a New Ethic*, trans. E. Rolfe, Shambhala Publications, 1990.

Tozzi, C. (2023) *Active Imagination in Theory, Practice and Training. The Special Legacy of C.G. Jung*. Routledge, Taylor & Francis.

von Franz, M.L. *L'immaginazione attiva secondo C.G. Jung* [Active Imagination according to C.G. Jung] in F. De Luca Comandini and R. Mercurio (eds.), *L'Immaginazione Attiva* [Active Imagination], La biblioteca di Vivarum, Milan, 2002.

von Franz, M.L. *Methods of Treatment in Analytical Psychology*. Stuttgart: Verlag Adolf Bonz, pp. 88–99, 1980.

von Franz, M.L. *C.G. Jung, His Myth in Our Time*. Inner City Books, 1998.

Von Franz, M.L. *Psychotherapy*. Boston and London: Shambhala Publications, 2014.

Zoja, L. *Al di là delle intenzioni. Etica e analisi* [Beyond intentions. Ethics and analysis]. Bollati Boringhieri Editore, Torino [in Italian], 2011.

Chapter 5

Sandplay Therapy and Active Imagination

Eva Pattis Zoja

"I would love to slide into the sand myself . . ." The words of the patient sitting in front of the sandtray conveyed both longing and surprised amusement at the idea of completely immersing herself in the sandtray. It was as if she had dared allow herself to defy material reality and give space to a symbolic need, at least in her imagination. It was the desire to feel comfortingly embraced – almost as if unborn. In Sandplay Therapy, children repeatedly bury miniature figures in the sand and unbury them again, thereby experiencing countless cycles of metaphoric death and rebirth in their play. Each cycle brings new life forces, previously concealed in the unconscious, into consciousness.

Sand as a therapeutic instrument activates a whole range of experiences in which the inner and outer worlds interact with each other. In a patient's first sandplay sessions, it is a possibility for the analyst to initially offer sand and water as the only two elements. This affords the patient the opportunity to experience a form of imagination that could be called kinaesthetic, in which every gesture, no matter how seemingly insignificant, can reveal a symbolic effect. Repetitions occur, but without any mechanical aspect to them; instead, they have a liberating effect, as if something as yet unperceived by consciousness were being celebrated. The elements of sand and water appear to connect us with a pre-cultural memory that leads us to perform actions without premeditation; and though we may not understand the meaning of these actions, they benefit us none the less.

Patients who are guided to touch the surface of the sand with their eyes closed often experience the sand as feeling unexpectedly soft. "I can't believe it, the sand is responding . . .," said one patient as she gently stroked its surface. It felt as if she were touching the skin of a baby. After a while, she looked me in the eyes and said with a smile, "I would like to have been caressed like that." There was no sadness in her voice, but the joy of discovery. She had perceived her action and experience merging into one: as she was caressing the sand, it felt as if she, too, were being caressed – and in a way that she had scarcely experienced before.

We can assume that the hands' impulses to move in the sandtray are analogous to the visually imagined images of Jung's classical Active Imagination. The parallels are apparent. According to Jung's instructions, Active Imagination consists of four successive stages, the first of which is to wait without intent until an image appears

DOI: 10.4324/9781003411369-5

before the inner eye, and to observe whether it then changes of its own accord. A very similar direction can be given in sandplay: to concentrate with closed eyes on perceiving the contact of the palms of the hands with the sand, then to focus inwards on any impulse to move that may present itself. If a visual image should appear, then it is not represented in the sand for the time being. If a patient's attention is confined to this inward sensorial focus for some time, this opens up access to deeper layers of the psyche, and the patient can explore not only pre-lingual but also pre-symbolic parts of his or her biography. Provided the conditions of a free and protected space and the presence of a person capable of empathy are met, the psyche will produce with almost somnambulistic certainty precisely what it needs at that moment: that which is under-represented in the consciousness. C.G. Jung called this the *compensatory function* of the psyche.

Thus it is possible, for example, that people who were born prematurely experience an unpleasant coolness or even a distinct coldness when they touch the sand for the first time, which may startle them. It is as if the psyche were "determined" to raise this first, difficult relationship of a prematurely born infant with its environment into consciousness, so that it can subsequently be processed and integrated. Instead of remaining split off and perhaps only making itself felt as an unexpectedly occurring state of anxiety, this early experience of panic becomes an integrative part of one's personal biography. It is revealing to observe how patients confront this unpleasant first contact with the sand in the course of the session. Some patients turn their back on the sandtray and prefer to talk. The unexpected perception of coldness is often followed by fear and also sadness, and patients speak about experiences from their childhood or even their current life – the theme being abandonment and vulnerability. One client immediately and palpably put his capacity for resilience into practice: he begin to warm the sand with his hands. Because the sand does indeed get warmer through the touch of the hands, this gave the client a sense of satisfaction and self-efficacy. The entire first sandplay session was to be passed in this manner, with the sand being warmed little by little, all the way to the furthest corners of the sandtray. The healing effect of such a ceremonial gesture is self-evident. All that is required of the therapist is attentive testimony and recognition of the self-regulation that the psyche has just accomplished. If one compares this action with Active Imagination as described by Jung, it becomes clear that – in a certain sense – the second and even third of the phases he describes have already taken place here: conscious confrontation of the unconscious. Jung recommends drawing or painting the experienced content in the third stage. We can see with our small example that the first three of the four phases of classical Active Imagination have been joined into a single action. The experience of coldness, which had spontaneously risen from the unconscious, was consciously confronted by an acting ego, which in turn initiated a transformation of the situation. The fact that the three phases occur almost simultaneously adds great emotional intensity while, at the same time, the rhythm of the repeated motions often has a deeply calming effect. Like a toddler managing to calm itself down.

The fourth phase described by Jung, on the other hand, takes place on a cognitive level: drawing the ethical conclusions from the newly attained level of consciousness. Whether in the practice of Active Imagination or in sandplay, this phase consists of a retrospective conscious reflection on the experience.

The following is another example of imagination with the help of the hands, this time emphasising the perception of space. As long as a patient sat at the sandtray with her eyes closed, the available space inside the tray struck her as enormous. The patient joyfully let her hands glide over the sand and took delight in its expanse. Her hands could move freely as if there were no boundaries. But as soon she opened her eyes, the sandtray became very tight. "How can it be so small? There's no room at all." The difference was so striking that she repeatedly opened and closed her eyes to try to fathom this remarkable change. The vastness she had perceived with her closed eyes represented an as yet unconscious potential of her psyche, whereas the sandtray's actual expanse reflected her real life, which was constricted by habits and in which she rarely allowed herself anything new. This observation came from the patient herself. She had concretely experienced a manifestation of her inner conflict, and had understood its meaning. This had an immediate and lasting effect on her. Above all, she was amazed at the ability of her own psyche to even produce something so "playful". Similar to how we are sometimes surprised and fascinated by the wisdom of a dream. The compensatory tendency of the psyche reveals itself in subtle ways, especially in sandplay.

Here is another example. A patient, eyes closed, had placed her hand on the surface of the sand and remained like that for a while, motionless. Slowly, her facial expression began to reveal that she was very moved by something. She began to cry. She explained that it was the first time she had felt something so solid under her hand. Something that "held" her, that she could hold on to, and that she could entrust herself to. In fact, it was only the raised sand that had formed under the palm of her hand. This little mound was the imprint of her own hand, and it fitted perfectly. One could say that this experience had taken place in a transitional space as described by D. Winnicott. Inside the sandtray everything can become a transitional object, just like the familiar examples of a child's security blanket or indispensable teddy bear: children encounter this object, but at the same time they have also created it. The inner and outer worlds become one.

One difference between Sandplay Therapy and Active Imagination is that the images that arise before the inner eye in Active Imagination are only concretely expressed in retrospect: they are drawn, painted or moulded. In sandplay, on the other hand, the unconscious contents are *themselves created* by means of the hands. Sometimes a patient may have the impression that an imagined being is actually coming towards him from the sandtray. Faces from the sandbox look up at him and reveal psychic elements that he had not previously been aware of.

Another difference between Active Imagination and Sandplay Therapy is that Sandplay Therapy takes place in the presence of the therapist, while Active Imagination was given to patients by C.G. Jung as a form of homework. Although sandplay takes place during the therapy session, it in no way resembles the various forms of guided imagination. Nothing is predetermined and there is no guidance from the therapist. It is the utter lack of intent which distinguishes Sandplay Therapy and Active Imagination. Both approaches are more akin to a creative process. The instructions to Active Imagination emphasise that the image sequences should not be imagined randomly. Jung recommends to carefully avoid jumping from one subject to another. He further emphasises that it is essential to approach the emerging contents, figures and situations as if they were real. This is why Active Imagination is a strenuous and rather slow process. The connections to concrete reality must be re-established again and again. In Sandplay Therapy, this aspect is already provided from the outset: the sand offers material resistance of its own accord – it can be moist, hard and resistant, or it can simply slip away. Jung advises offering Active Imagination only to those patients whose ego complexes are strong enough to actively face the arising unconscious contents and their associated emotions. Such caution is not needed in sandplay as long as the therapist keeps an eye on the patient's motivation. People with a fragile ego complex are usually not drawn to sandplay in the first place; they find the many miniature figures confusing, the sand seems too loose, not compact enough. If a therapist listens carefully and does not try to force things, the psyche is able to distinguish very precisely what is good for it and what is not.

In the following I would like to show how psychic content that has been split off from consciousness or repressed can surface in bodily sensations by means of sandplay. One patient had first closed her eyes, placed her palms on the sand and started to enclose some sand in her fists. She repeatedly gathered sand in her fists, enjoyed holding it for a long time, then let go of the sand again so as to pick up some more. After a while, however, she became impatient and frustrated; she felt that her hands were actually much too small and that they could therefore only hold very little sand. She said she would like to experience the feeling of holding much larger amounts of sand in her fists. She added, irritably, that she had the fists of a child. Little by little, she became painfully aware that the metaphorical level of this feeling corresponded with her day-to-day experience: she suffered from the impression of not being able to meet her environment's demands, and an underlying feeling of incompetence had accompanied her for decades. She criticised herself on the inside and selectively heard criticism in the comments of her fellow human beings. We spoke about the possibility of taking this image of small fists, which the body and psyche had so clearly produced, seriously, and finding out what function such an image could have for her. Could it be that her everyday actions were indeed influenced by a childlike immaturity? I drew the patient's attention to the fact that small fists simply couldn't help being small, that they perhaps suffered from constant excessive demands and maybe wanted nothing more than to be seen and respected as small by the patient herself. Then it occurred to the woman that she had always regarded herself as a power woman who could do everything on her own and didn't need anyone's help. And that at the same time she was often disappointed that almost nobody cared for her, even in situations where her need for help was clear, such as when she had broken a foot: neither her family nor her friends had offered help. "She's so strong, she'll manage just fine," seemed to be the others' motto. The stark contrast between this and the little fists had now become obvious, and it was also clear to us that it must create an exhausting tension in her life, which was reflected in phases of listlessness. From then on, the "little fists" became a catchword in her therapy, they helped her become more patient with herself and to gradually accept her childlike sides, thus allowing them to mature.

Both methods, Active Imagination and Sandplay Therapy, promote what Theodor Reik (1888–1969) has called *Listening with the Third Ear*. The therapeutic effect of this attempt to patiently and carefully listen inward, to gradually sense what is appearing in front of the inner eye or in the sandtray, cannot be overstated. Therefore, the actual content of the imagination or of what is created in sandplay is not even that important. The mere fact that *anything* appears that exists beyond all expectations, reactions and opinions is invaluable. Both methods readily and directly activate our innate capacity for resilience.

During verbal therapy sessions, we often observe that a patient's hands appear eager to get involved – either they pick at things nervously or they interlock in a tense way. In such cases, the invitation to sit down at the sandtray and continue talking there is often perceived as a great relief. What follows is often striking to therapist and patient alike: the patient's way of speaking is changed, the voice becomes deeper and calmer, the words better chosen, there is more time for breaths between sentences, and more pauses. It is as if the patient is only now listening to him- or herself. This would mean that the hands' contact with the sand had opened up a new dialogical, inner space. People suffering from panic attacks do not have such an inner, dialogical space. If they can be brought to talk to themselves imaginatively, then this is a first step towards overcoming the panic. The panic-inducing notion is ultimately always the experience of being lost alone in the universe. But if one can manage to say to oneself, "Now just make yourself a cup of tea . . .," then an inner relational space is opened up, in which conflicts can be dealt with. Active Imagination and Sandplay Therapy both focus on developing this inner relational space.

Chapter 6

Imaginative Movement Therapy

A Neo-Jungian Approach to Active Imagination

Laner Cassar

Imaginative Movement Therapy (IMT) is an attempt to try to dream Jung's method of Active Imagination forward in today's world. Jung's *Red Book* (2009) still offers us today a much needed inspiring guide of how to explore one's inner realms in the face of dooming angst and a cold alienation of the spirit of our times, yet the path it presents may be daunting to the average denizen or patient. As a result, IMT tries to address this concern by facilitating the patient's process to have a more personal experience of one's depths. Unlike the classical use of Active Imagination where the latter is done alone, IMT takes a relational form and is practised in the presence of a therapist. IMT offers a different and more benevolent kind of descent into that nether realm, unlike the myth of Persephone and her abduction by Hades into the underworld. In IMT, the therapist takes more of Hermes' role as that of psycho-pomp who leads us to think about the underworld experience in a particular way, and his approach is one of being guided to rather than abducted to the underworld. The therapist also helps the patient to develop a capacity to imagine (if this is lacking) as well as a symbolic attitude, thus respecting the most important aspect of Active Imagination, beyond any form it may take, namely of having "an attitude towards the unconscious" (Singer, 1972, p. 343).[1] Because of its more or less established setting and relative guidance by the therapist, IMT comes across as more accessible than Jung's Active Imagination while ensuring that it is less directive than Desoille's Directed Waking Dream method (Desoille, 1938, 1945).

IMT stands out as a hybridised-integrative therapeutic modality developed from Jung's Active Imagination and Robert Desoille's Directed Waking Dream (*Rêve éveillé dirigé* – RED), two imaginative approaches that were developed in Europe in the first decades of the twentieth century, separately from each other. IMT enriches C.G. Jung's analytical psychology with Desoille's Directed Waking Dream method while respecting the tenets of analytical psychology. It was developed and pioneered by myself as part of my doctoral research in psychoanalytic studies (Cassar, 2014, 2016, 2020). In IMT, the less-known French *Rêve éveillé dirigé* method serves as the other, as well as the shadow of the Active Imagination technique. Desoille's Directed Waking Dream serves as an initial stimulus for active imagination itself so as to enable it to engage in a self-reflexive process. Qualities such as the therapist's guidance vs. auto-guidance, directiveness vs. spontaneity,

DOI: 10.4324/9781003411369-6

movement of image vs. staying long with one image, relaxation and body ground-ing vs. absence of relaxation, brief vs. long-term work and by-passing vs. work-ing through resistance, challenge us to look at active imagination differently. IMT allows Active Imagination to reclaim and integrate certain disowned and split-off aspects. Jung (2009) ended *The Red Book* with an unfinished 1959 epilogue with a final word that is the noun *Möglichkeit*, which in German means possibility. IMT is an attempt to develop such new possibilities. Ironically, IMT fulfils Desoille's wish to collaborate with Jung, at least posthumously, since Desoille's gesture to reach Jung by sending him a signed copy of his 1938 book (still in Jung's own library) was not reciprocated (ibid., 2020).

The imaginative experience in IMT is called a "waking dream" and it refers to a guided exploration of one's inner reality through imagination. Imagination in an IMT "waking dream" enters the world of metaphor. Imagination can be viewed as providing a symbolic bridge between our conscious and unconscious thoughts. Ul-timately, it gives us a platform for expression and offers a wide array of tools with which to understand ourselves at greater depth. The waking dream gives the patient the opportunity to journey wilfully and sensorially through a world that embod-ies their belief systems, which are discovered in the form of images. The patient, known as the adventurer, traveller or pilgrim/seeker, pauses from his or her real life and enters an atemporal mythical one, echoing Coleridge's most famous phrase of a "willing suspension of disbelief" (Coleridge, 1817/1907, p. 6).[2] Thus, it is not the usual guided imagery we use to relax, or the creative visualisation or mental rehearsal, or role-plays we engage in, to win a match or pass an interview. The word "imaginative" in IMT distinguishes imaginative from imaginary. This echoes Jung's distinction of passive fantasy and active fantasy. For Jung, passive fantasy is a subjective figment of the mind while active fantasy is an image-making, form-creative activity. In his distinction of terms, he seemed to have been following the medieval alchemists who emphasised the difference between daydreams and crea-tive imagination or *phantasia* and *imaginatio*. In fact, in *The Tavistock Lectures* Jung equates active fantasy with imagination proper "per veram imaginationem et non phantastica" and explains that fantasy is "mere nonsense" while imagina-tion is "active purposeful creation" (Jung, 1935/1976, p. 171 [CW18, para. 396].[3] More recently, Coleman (2006), like in IMT, also distinguishes real imagination from passive fantasy. Nonetheless, even passive fantasy can also be deepened and explored for its defensive purposes.

The word "movement" in IMT, besides referring to both the explorative move-ment and resting of the imaginal-body ego in the imaginative landscape, refers to the fact that when we visualise or imagine, we also stimulate the neuromuscular circuitry, thus engaging a body response even when lying down. Bachelard argued that a waking dream, contrary to the psychoanalytic method, offers "*une mise en marche*/a way forward" (Bachelard, 1943, pp. 130–145).[4] The same can be said of IMT. The waking dreams in IMT offer an introverted facilitated "pilgrimage". Instead of aiming at a spiritual transformation it aims for an emotional metamor-phosis of the inner wandering "pilgrim". It helps the patient through his or her impasse, towards a personal evolution and transformation, since the aim of the therapy is not primarily an exploration of the past. IMT Therapy aims to facilitate the movement of imagery in imaginary time and space, as an efficient means to access dissociated unconscious material both from the personal, unrepressed and collective unconscious. IMT uses imagination to tap into unconscious material so as to unblock the patient's creativity. The waking dream is in fact another royal road to the unconscious. IMT is mainly used with adults but can be adapted to children as well as used for group therapy. It is used with patients experiencing normal developmental problems as well as with some patients with some personality disorders but not with psychotics.

The main steps of this therapeutic procedure are represented by the acronym RIPE; namely, *R*elaxation, *I*nduction, *P*rompting & reparation, and *E*laboration and interpretation. There is also a final stage on Negotiation (N), which invites the patient to see which aspects are and can be integrated into his or her life. These steps are grouped on three Arts, namely:

- The art of Relaxation and Inducing a waking dream
- The art of Prompting and Reparation
- The art of Symbolic Elaboration and Interpretation.

During the Relaxation stage the therapist invites the patient-seeker to find a relaxed position in an armchair or couch (facing the therapist) and to focus on his or her breathing. Then the patient is given an initial verbal stimulus known as "*enargeic*" stimuli to start a waking dream. *Enargeic* comes from the Greek rhetorical term *enargeia*.[5] The initial stimulus allows the patient to enter an imaginative landscape and to position himself or herself in it and to describe out loud to the therapist what he or she is experiencing in this imaginative space. A spontaneous image from the client may serve as a point of departure. Other ego-syntonic stimuli that serve the same purpose are metaphors, symbols from nocturnal dreams, daydreams or waking dreams, sensations in the body, results from psychological projective tests like the Word Association Test or the Thematic Apperception Test, patients' drawings, or from those pictures in the therapist's office to which the patient is naturally drawn in a particular instance, or from the therapist's counter-transference. The therapist may also choose stimuli geared at a specific purpose, like classical Jungian verbal stimuli to access the shadow aspect of the personal unconscious. This may range from entering a cave, cellar or forest, opening a trap door or exploring a shipwreck, amongst others.

The second stage is known as the Prompting and Reparation stage. The therapist asks the patient to immerse himself or herself in the imaginative landscape and to see himself or herself in it through a self-representation known as imaginative-body ego. The therapist invites the patient to have a sensorial experience of whatever he or she is imagining, i.e. to describe with all the senses, the colours, sounds, smells of whatever he or she encounters and to voice it to the therapist as an *ekphrastic*[6] narrative. The latter serves the purpose of elaborating the oneiric drama by suffusing it with the patient's creativity, and to allow for recall and reinterpretation of the key images, emotions and acts within the oneiric journey. The waking dream reflects the accomplishment of a stage of significant confidence between patient and therapist, that requires prior sessions of work to achieve.

Certain personality styles might be more or less amenable to the process of initiating a waking dream. The paranoid might approach the request defensively as if it were an invasion of mental privacy. The obsessional might demonstrate an overactive dependence on the pragmatic and logical that impedes free associative powers and imagination. The schizoid might find it easier to speak through a waking dream than directly to the therapist. While the histrionic and dependent might find that the attention of the therapist is invested heavily into this component of the psychotherapeutic model, and might attempt to elaborate unnecessarily in an effort to please, or to add a dramatic touch to the material being imagined. The IMT practitioner has to find creative ways to encourage the patient to have a genuine and authentic experience, rather than hide behind controlling defences.

Besides the role of helping the patient to start and to enter a waking dream, the therapist can also make use of prompting interventions such as to move and explore the imaginative landscape or else to rest if the patient needs to do so. The therapist encourages the patient to interact with objects and figures encountered. The therapist also monitors the anxiety levels in the oneirodrama and offers grounding interventions to support the patient when faced with anxious and overwhelming encounters. As such, prompting should limit itself to generic suggestions when obstacles are encountered. Heracles, Orpheus and the Sibyl of Cumae all had to face Cerberus, and managed to overcome him with strength, song and sops, respectively.

These prompting interventions by the therapist to the patient immersed in his or her waking dream are summarised in the CAR model:

C: *Confronting.* Here confrontation does not refer to challenging aggressively the figures encountered, but is about encouraging the patient to interact, dialogue, get closer, feed and touch unconscious figures.
A: *Affective experiencing.* While the patient is exploring sensorially the oneiric landscape, he or she is also asked to check his or her feelings.
R: *Reparation.* The therapist-guide can also support or remind the patient about the use of certain resources or abilities he or she possesses that might be useful to navigate the dangerous landscape or face frightening figures.

The oneirodrama takes from 5 to 15 minutes. It takes longer when the patient becomes accustomed to it and can relax and immerse himself or herself in the waking dream. Since in a waking dream you enter a mytho-poetic space, time seems to stop and the natural duration of time is distorted.

A short vignette can help to understand better the stages of starting and entering a waking dream as well as the art of prompting. A male patient with a dependent personality was experiencing heaviness in his life in general and depressive feelings since he had decided to leave an abusive relationship with a female partner which he experienced as controlling. He found himself still interacting with her from time to time since he was still afraid of her. I asked him what does he carry within him that was weighing him down. He did not know how to answer. I then probed again as an image arose in my counter-transference. I asked him if he had to close his eyes and imagine opening a heavy chest with discarded things which were not pleasant, what would he fantasise about finding?

My patient closed his eyes and after some time started to speak. He said: "I am seeing a lot of rotten leaves and smelling a foul smell. The once green vegetation has died in the cellar I am in." "What made the vegetation die?", I asked. He answered: "The gardener left it without taking care of it and as a result it died. The gardener has been busy with other important things and forgot about tending to the vegetation." End of waking Dream. He felt sad and fell silent.

Then the patient recalled how, as a child, his parents had been very busy and he was not given the attention he needed, and as an adult he craved it but seemed to be looking for it in the wrong people. He had also developed altruistic coping defences which cut him off from his own inner "nature", so as to avoid feeling the heaviness of loss and withdrawal of love in his life. Subsequent sessions also used the image of the gardener as a starting point for a waking dream so as to be able to dialogue with this figure.

After the patient finishes describing his or her *ekphrastic* narrative (as in the case just described), the therapist invites the patient to write and/or draw the content of their waking dream as well as their associations to it. The therapist also invites the patient to bring this again to the next session where the patient and therapist elaborate on and amplify the symbolic content of the material. Interpretation is done from a teleological and prospective point of view.

A symbol can have many meanings and be interpreted in many ways. The meanings of a symbol are profound and transcend time, but, as noted above, the particular meaning a symbol has depends in part on the personal associations the dreamer assigns to it. However, the oneiric experience itself, i.e. the waking dream, can also be beneficial on its own accord in IMT since there is an unblocking of unexpressed emotions and a confrontation with dissociated complexes. IMT functions through an intermodal expressive and analytical model since it allows the patient to express in his or her imagination unconscious content as well as think about the contents experienced in an analytical way. In IMT the therapist looks at the waking dream in terms of the following points:

1 Landscape/setting – nature, buildings, underwater, higher grounds, celestial . . .
2 Atmosphere – dark, light . . .
3 Key figures – from personal unconscious (animals) or from collective unconscious (mythical or celestial figures)
4 Presence and quality of imaginal-body ego
5 Direction – up or down, right or left, forwards or backwards
6 Quality of interaction with the landscape: move acts and expressive acts
7 Levels of passivity and activity

8 Themes – repeated themes in the waking dreams
9 The main emotions of the oneiric experience as described by the patient and as observed by the therapist
10 Prospective elements for the future
11 Duration of the waking dream
12 Entry point and exit point, including sudden interruption
13 Quality of the non-verbals (pauses, soft voice . . .) in the *ekphrastic* narrative
14 Response by nocturnal dreams in between sessions
15 Censoring/use of defences in description of key content of the waking dream in the written report of the patient.

Some of the above points are similar to nocturnal dream interpretation or image interpretation as explained by Jung and Freud but some are more specific to the waking dream methodology given it is done in the presence of the therapist. While Freud thought that dreams expressed forbidden wishes that had to be disguised (he differentiated the manifest content of a dream – what was on the surface, from the latent content – what was hidden), Jung saw dreams as expressing things openly. Jung (1954) wrote: "They do not deceive, they do not lie, they do not distort or disguise . . . They are invariably seeking to express something that the ego does not know and does not understand" (CW17, para. 189).[7]

The therapist and the patient collaboratively explore the actions of the patient in the waking dream, which can follow the linguistic model of transitivity. Some actions are transitively performed by the patient onto an object in the waking dream, such as feeding an animal, throwing a stone or opening a door. The symbolic elaboration can focus on the state of the transitive object before and after the action demonstrated by the client's imagined self. Thus, a door which was closed and now lies open after the patient's imaginal-body ego opens it, shows the patient's interactivity and immersion in the oneiric landscape. The intransitive movements of the patient in the waking dream are also grist for the interpretative mill. The physical acts of walking, running, jumping, flying and even sitting still, can reflect the energy level and curiosity of the patient. Allowing for, and observing, the movements can be both a diagnostic measure of the current emotional and psychological state of the patient, as well as a therapeutic consent for the patient to explore movements that may not usually be part of his or her standard repertoire.

After a waking dream experience, the therapist also invites the patient to be aware of any dream or dreams he or she might have had in between sessions which might confirm, dismiss or add to the material reflected upon in the session dedicated to elaborating the symbolic material of the waking dream. Thus a dialectic is created between waking dreams and nocturnal dreams. This also gives the IMT method a broader therapeutic scope beyond the practising of a technique.

Before we provide a waking dream experience, we need to make a good anamnesis of the patient, a thorough assessment of their personality, and have a good idea of the kind of problem presented. Also, with some patients, you first need to teach them how to use their imagination. Furthermore, it is imperative to provide a safe sheltering space (container or alchemical vessel) and build a good working alliance with the patient. The therapist should support the patient, take care of their safety and remain vigilant. The required space should provide the release of Ego- and Self-defences so that the unconscious material will enter the space.

In some cases, clients who are very anxious will respond well to being given a relaxation exercise, starting with the muscles and then the breathing, such as progressive muscle relaxation or autogenic training. This is more crucial with trau- matised patients. Jung also speaks of the importance of stilling the mind to allow unconscious material to emerge. In fact, in his essay "The Transcendent Func- tion", Jung wrote: "The capacity to produce free fantasies can, however, be de- veloped with practice. The training consists first of all in systematic exercises for eliminating critical attention, thus producing a vacuum in consciousness" (Jung, 1916/1960, p. 77 [CW8, para. 155]).[8] The relaxation helps to create a bridge for the waking dream to connect better psyche with soma. It also helps the patient to give attention to his or her body prior to entering the waking dream and thus to be able to stay connected with it whilst the oneiric drama leads the patient to experience different emotions, some of which may be difficult to face.

With other patients, sometimes the therapist can seize the moment and start a waking dream by honing in on good metaphors brought by the patient, a spontane- ous image or part of a dream. In such cases it is enough to ask the patient to be more comfortable, close his or her eyes, breathe in and out and see what comes to his or her mind as the therapist gives the patient initial *enargeic* and ego-syntonic stimuli.

The *enargeic* stimulus, which is usually verbal but can also be auditory, tactile, visual or olfactory, helps free the patient's imaginative experience leading to a *drame interieur*, involving an unfolding of what urgently seeks expression. The stimulus is a powerful and direct route into the imaginal and the way can lead to all possible scenarios . . . everything is possible . . . the imaginal ego can walk, swim, climb and even fly. In "The Transcendent Function", Jung (1916/1960) observed:

[W]e find cases where there is no tangible mood or depression at all, but just a general dull discontent, a feeling of resistance to everything, a sort of boredom or vague disgust, an indefinable but excruciating emptiness. In these cases no definite starting point exists – it would first have to be created.

(Jung, 1958/1960, p. 83 [CW8, para. 169])[9]

IMT caters for such scenarios as described by Jung but about which he hardly gave any more detail. This approach, in contrast to Jung's Active Imagination, provides an element of guidance, but the stimuli are nevertheless usually coming from the patient, hence ego-syntonic stimuli. If the patient cannot come up with anything, the therapist can choose a stimulus from nature such as imagining you are walking through a path in nature, or along the sea or stream, or in a green space to which you have never been. These will serve to unlock the patient's imagination and also to strengthen the patient's ego. Moreover, they can give us clues about the patient's inner psychic landscapes in terms of resources, or lack of them. Such horizontal stimuli are safer to start with before diving to the depths or flying to celestial heights.

One of the roles of the therapist is to facilitate the imaginative journey of the patient and to make the best of it. Dante had Virgil in the *Divine Comedy* while Jung had Philemon in his *Red Book*. A teacher, or guide, is essential. If one needs a guide to cross an unknown land, how much more does one need a guide to help one through the unknown inner world.

As Rûmi said, we have to choose a master, for without one this journey is full of tribulations, fears and dangers and that, with no escort, one would be lost on a road one would have already taken. Likewise in IMT, we do not travel alone. Like a tour guide, the therapist asks the patient to bring him- or herself with his or her *imaginal-body ego* in the imaginative landscape and to experience it. The therapist prompts the patient-seeker further into movement, into exploration and into facing his or her inner self. To do so, he or she needs to develop these seven therapeutic competencies, namely:

1 *Attunement competence* – Knowing what is happening in the moment and what is making the therapist want to introduce a waking dream in that particular moment.
2 *Knowledge competence* – Having skills on how to start and guide a waking dream as well as how to elaborate it.
3 *Therapeutic confidence competence* – Having the confidence to help a patient engage with a waking dream, immerse himself or herself in it and knowing how to offer support when needed.
4 *Negative capability competence* – Knowing how to stay with uncertainty when the oneirodrama is unfolding and not to be too intrusive in the waking dream.
5 *Determination competence* – How to not to give up from the beginning when the patient shows signs of reluctance or shyness to engage in a waking dream.
6 *Braking competence* – How the therapist must be attentive and respectful and not push the patient to continue at any cost.
7 *Experiential process competence* – How the therapist has to observe what is happening to the patient and to work with it and around it.

The therapist guides the patient to enter the imaginative landscape and to immerse himself or herself in it with all his or her senses. The therapist encourages the patient to engage and make contact with any figures and objects encountered along his or her inner journey. This is known as confrontation. Confronting is in line with Jungian psychology. Viewing confrontation as engagement, rather than aggression or conflict, is consistent with Jung's (1995) analytic perspective, which valued the importance of confrontation to the analytic process, having referred to his own descent experience during the years from 1913 through 1917 as his "confrontation with the unconscious".[10] By confronting their own frightening imagery, the patient can overcome their fears, and they would have desensitized themselves to a part of their own personality to which they have been rather allergic. In these circumstances, many atimes the frightening image often spontaneously changes to something less threatening. When the patient is very anxious in front of certain figures encountered, the therapist encourages the patient to ground himself or herself or to seek other safe ways in which to support oneself. These encounters can then be reflected upon and elaborated in the next face-to-face session where associations of the symbolic material are done. Usually in a two-year course of psychotherapy, an average of 20 waking dreams can be done with the patient and reflected upon together, as part of other unconscious material which emerges in therapy such as from nocturnal dreams or drawings.

The IMT therapist has to be very skilled in guiding the patient and is called to make his or her own personal therapeutic process using the imagination so as to be aware of the patient's experience when having a waking dream. This will make them aware of their personal blind spots which can interfere in their therapeutic work. Supervision is also needed to support the therapist's work with his or her patients. Basic and advanced training in this methodology is offered to practising professionals in the field of counselling, psychology and psychotherapy.

In IMT, the therapist not only witnesses but actively facilitates the patient to get in touch with unconscious material. This method emphasises the principles of facilitation, exploration, expression, holding, reciprocity, affective resonance and communicable meaning. IMT can offer practical ideas to Jungian practitioners of how to use active imagination in the therapy session. This methodology can help close the gap in certain Jungian institutes around the world, where Active Imagination does not feature prominently in the teaching or practise of Jungian analysts as evidenced by Tozzi's (2023)[11] international research on Active Imagination. IMT's framework fits in within a mytho-poetic therapeutic approach where analysis co-operates with poetic-imaginative reflection. IMT also adds an experiential approach of movement, characteristic of Desoille's Directed Waking Dream method, besides one of dialogue which is usually associated with Active Imagination. IMT can thus be promoted and included amongst the Jungian expressive arts modalities which derive from Jung's active imagination, such as art therapy, drama therapy, dance/movement therapy, play and sandplay therapy. This new therapeutic modality can also give the visual approach of doing active imagination a proper framework in the expressive arts.

Conclusion

Through this chapter the reader becomes familiar with the three main Arts of Imaginative Movement therapy, namely: the art of starting a waking dream, the art of prompting and reparative interventions, and the art of symbolic elaboration and interpretation. These three Arts help to position IMT as a neo-Jungian approach to Carl Jung's Active Imagination. While integrating aspects from Desoille's Directed Waking Dream Method, IMT strives to remain true to the spirit of Analytical psychology by underlying the therapeutic competencies required by the therapist-guide who accompanies the patient-traveller in his or her exploration of his or her inner unconscious landscape revealed in the waking dream. Nonetheless, IMT's key aspects of facilitation and relationality remain in the service of the unfolding psyche in search of renewal and continued transformation.

Notes

1 Singer, J. (1972). *Boundaries of the Soul: The Practice of Jung's Psychology*. Garden City, NY: Anchor Books.
2 Coleridge, S.T. (1907). *Biographia literaria*. London: Oxford University Press. Originally published in 1817.
3 Jung, C.G. (1976). The Tavistock lectures: On the theory and practice of analytical psychology. In W. McGuire (Exec. Ed.), Sir H. Read, M. Fordham, & G. Adler (Eds.), *Collected Works Volume 18: The Symbolic Life* (R. F. C. Hull, Trans.). (pp. 5–182). Princeton, NJ: Princeton University Press. Originally published in 1935.
4 See Bachelard, G. (1943). *L'air et les songes: essai sur l'imagination du movement* [Air and dreams: Essay on the imagination of movement]. Paris: Librairie Jose Corti.
5 The Greek rhetorical term *enargeia* refers to a visually powerful description that vividly recreates something or someone in words.
6 The Greek word *ekphrasis* refers to the use of detailed description of a work of visual art as a literary device, in our case the spoken waking dream narrative.
7 Jung, C.G. (1954). Analytical psychology and education (Lecture Two). In W. McGuire (Exec. Ed.), Sir H. Read, M. Fordham, & G. Adler (Eds.), *Collected Works Volume 17: The Development of Personality* (R.F.C. Hull, Trans.). (pp. 81–107). Princeton, NJ: Princeton University Press. (Originally published in 1946.)
8 Jung, C.G. (1960). The transcendent function. In H. Read, M. Fordham, G. Adler, & W. McGuire (Eds.), *Collected Works Volume 8: The Structure and the Dynamics of the Psyche* (R.F.C. Hull. Trans.) (pp. 67–91). New York: Bollingen Foundation. Originally published in 1916.
9 Ibid. para 169, p. 83.
10 Jung, C.G. (1995). *Memories, Dreams, Reflections*. London: Fontana Press. (Originally published in 1963.)
11 Tozzi, C. (2023). *Active Imagination in Theory, Practice and Training. The Special Legacy of C.G. Jung*. London and New York: Routledge, Taylor & Francis.

References

Bachelard, G. (1943). *L'air et les songes: essai sur l'imagination du movement* [Air and dreams: Essay on the imagination of movement]. Paris: Librairie Jose Corti.

Cassar, L. (2014). Shades of RED – Jung's Technique in the Red Book and Desoille's R.E.D (Rêve éveillé dirigé) Method. In *Proceedings of the XIXth International Congress for Analytical Psychology*. Copenhagen: Daimon.

Cassar, L. (2016). *Bridging Imaginative Pathways: Jung's Technique of Active Imagination and Desoille's Directed Waking Dream Method*. PhD thesis, Centre for Psychoanalytic Studies, University of Essex, UK.

Cassar, L. (2020). *Jung's Technique of Active Imagination and Desoille's Directed Waking Dream Method: Bridging the Divide*. London: Routledge.

Coleman, W. (2006). Imagination and the imaginary. *Journal of Analytical Psychology*, *51*(1), 21–41.

Coleridge, S.T. (1907). *Biographia literaria*. London: Oxford University Press. (Originally published in 1817.)

Desoille, R. (1938). *Exploration de l'affectivité subconsciente par la méthode du rêve éveillé: sublimation et acquisitions psychologiques* [An exploration of the subconscious emotions through the waking dream method: Sublimation and psychological acquistions]. Paris: J.L.L. D'Artrey.

Desoille, R. (1945). *Le rêve éveillé en psychothérapie: Essai sur la fonction de régulation de l'inconscient collectif* [The waking dream in psychotherapy: Essay on the regulatory function of the collective unconscious]. Paris: Presses universitaires de France.

Jung, C.G. (1954). Analytical psychology and education (Lecture Two). In W. McGuire (Exec. Ed.), Sir H. Read, M. Fordham, & G. Adler (Eds.). *Collected Works Volume 17: The Development of Personality*. (R.F.C. Hull, Trans.) (pp. 81–107). Princeton, NJ: Princeton University Press. (Originally published in 1946.)

Jung, C. G. (1960). The transcendent function. In H. Read, M. Fordham, G. Adler, & W. McGuire (Eds.), *Collected Works Volume 8: The Structure and the Dynamics of the Psyche* (R. F. C. Hull. Trans.). (pp. 67–91). New York: Bollingen Foundation. (Originally published in 1916).

Jung, C.G. (1976). The Tavistock lectures: On the theory and practice of analytical psychology. In W. McGuire (Exec. Ed.), Sir H. Read, M. Fordham, & G. Adler (Eds.), *Collected Works Volume 18: The Symbolic Life* (R.F.C. Hull, Trans.) (pp. 5–182). Princeton, NJ: Princeton University Press. (Originally published in 1935.)

Jung, C.G. (1995). *Memories, Dreams, Reflections*. London: Fontana Press. (Originally published in 1963.)

Jung, C.G. (2009). *The Red Book, Liber Novus*. (Ed. Sonu Shamdasani. Trans. Mark Kyburz, John Peck, & Sonu Shamdasani). New York: W.W Norton & Company.

Singer, J. (1972). *Boundaries of the Soul: The Practice of Jung's Psychology*. Garden City, NY: Anchor Books.

Tozzi, C. (2023). *Active Imagination in Theory, Practice and Training. The Special Legacy of C.G. Jung*. London and New York: Routledge, Taylor & Francis.

Chapter 7

The Magic Labyrinth

Imagine a Game to Be Played with Images

Valerio Colangeli

Introduction

Imagination and *imaginal thought* share numerous areas with *symbolic play*. We know, for example, how these functions play a fundamental role in the development of symbolic thinking in the child: if the imagination allows the child to process his own internal contents, "safely", through *pretending*,[1] playing establishes rules, boundaries, frames, but also motivation, passion, and the necessary energy for the *magic* to happen. Exactly like the *setting*, therefore, playing also fulfills the function of both the *Temenos* (the container, static, stable, and reliable over time) and the *Atanor* (the living and dynamic fire, which leads to action). The possibility of inventing *rules for each type of game* is the result of an ongoing process, which is determined in the relational field and to which analyst and patient give shape.

Despite these premises, in the context of analytical psychotherapy, techniques based on imaginal thought (such as Active Imagination), or on symbolic play (such as sandplay therapy), could not understandably be integrated at the operational level, remaining quite distinct from each other, both in terms of training and scientific dissemination. And I believe it is necessary, from a technical point of view, to differentiate and distinguish the various tools to avoid confusion and ambiguity in practice: for sure the object of investigation is always the unconscious, but one technique is to dialogue with it through dreams, another is to use active imagination, and yet another is to use sandplay. At the same time, however, we know that the fundamental tool of every therapist is his/her own personality.[2] Therefore, it will not only be the precision and correctness in the use of the specific tool that will be decisive, but the therapist's ability to combine his/her skills and knowledge (professional, personal, cultural, and more) *creatively*, in the encounter with the patient. This aspect will be fundamental in working analytically with teenagers, most of all because it allows the therapist and client to meet each other in a space on the edge of the adult's and child's world, encouraging and supporting them in their search for an identity and, at the same time, accepting and taking care of the suffering infant parts.

DOI: 10.4324/9781003411369-7

Active Imaginal Play: A Clinical Application

The Active Imaginal Play's Main Character

Massimo is a boy of almost 15 years old. He attends the second year of high school. In February 2021, he came to consultation because, since the Covid pandemic he has started to withdraw more and more, not connecting to the D.A.D. (distance learning), to the detriment of his academic performance. His mother, on the phone, tells me only that, despite having always been an introverted child, up to the seventh grade he had done well in school but that, in the last few months, he has inflicted cuts on his arms; at first, without saying anything to her. Massimo introduces himself, in the initial interviews, wearing a fisherman's hat, some glasses and a sweatshirt from Disney, studs and chokers as accessories; he looks smaller than his age. He is homosexual, and since he came out to his family his father has not been able to accept him, while his mother does not seem to give it too much importance, even if she insults him for how he dresses and for the people he associates with.

The mother, besides herself, tells of the perfect pregnancy of her first child, a daughter, who is now at university and doing well. She is a teacher, and she talks about her son as if he were one of her students, listing the scholastic shortcomings that have accentuated a distance between them, the problems that since childhood he has given them (such as long-term bedwetting). She says that M. "came out" in the seventh grade, leaking feelings of shame and anger, which confirm the harassing and devaluing experiences reported by M.

The father, since he learned of his son's homosexuality, has been depressed; he says that he understands it, but is worried because "these kids are being teased, attacked", while he would just like a "normal" life for his son. After the evaluation interviews, I agree to follow M. in psychotherapy, suggesting the parents start family therapy, and providing them with the contact details of a colleague. The parents don't think they can manage it because, in the past, family sessions have caused the father to have panic attacks.

We start the therapy, and, at the same time, M. is visited by a private psychiatrist who prescribes drugs therapy and overwhelms him with definitions and diagnoses.

1. Phase I: The Rule Book

1.1. Imagining the Session as a Game Space: From Images to PCs (Player Characters)

First of all, it will be useful to define a *game rule book* (setting) that allows us to be mobile within and rigorous in the frame, in the hope, as the sessions proceed, to *create a dream for the patient*, to be able to imagine his evolutionary change facilitating entry into its *proximal development zone*. In this way, play stimulates the *psyche's capacity for self-regulation*, which opens up to the idea of limitation and self-control within certain freely accepted boundaries; on a collective level it favors *civilization*, introducing the use of *rules* and the concept of *fairness*. Within these boundaries it's possible to stay with the images.

> *During the evaluation interviews, M. tells me about the cutting and says that he first did it because he couldn't cry, then "to feel himself", then because it gave him pleasure. The first "rule of the game" that we share, therefore, is precisely on self-cutting acts: we reflect about how cutting himself is a way of expressing certain things, and I urge him not to do it since he could try to express those things here, during the session. It seems to work and, in the following months, the episodes decrease in frequency until they disappear.*
>
> *The D.A.D. ends, school resumes with attendance in person, and Max would like to not go because he feels he can't manage it. I propose written contracts, weekly, signed by both of us, indicating the days (at least three) in which he must go to school, and it seems to work.*

Knowing how to keep the right distance (*mobile, variable,* and *malleable*), through the sharing of game rules, allows the patient to be able to approach his internal parts, in the form of characters not explicitly his own, just like in a video game, by immersing himself while still being able to go out whenever he wants.

1.2.   Waiting/Imagining PCs

Once the rules of the game have been settled, it will be possible to *stay with the emotions*, with the transference and countertransference experiences behind the acted out, still unapproachable, for the patient, at a level of consciousness. All this is necessary to give him back the possibility of staying in the change, however *catastrophic* it may be, without being destroyed by it, following the curiosity of wanting to know and enter his world, giving him the freedom to be able to look inside, in a process of self-discovery, to be able to face together, without haste.

> *Massimo, says his mother, was born after three abortions, in the same period of his paternal grandfather's death, in a situation permeated by pain and despair, with the fantasy and urgency of being able to return to life through Massimo. The feeling of meeting this family is distance, as if everyone lived their life and their emotions are closed within themselves, without seeing the other, unable to create an emotional contact and authentic communication. Parental expectations, moreover, of becoming "what he wants but without disappointing them", did not allow M. to stay in the change and emotions without being overwhelmed by them, so much fear of the threshold, of chaos, of every cut. During the interviews, it seems like he's not really there. For him, his symptoms speak, always described with impressionistic tones, with charged and irritating images:*

*self-harm, suicidal thoughts, hatred of everyone, depression, apathy, and abu-
lia. On the countertransference level it is all very tiring because M. embodies a
negative envy that does not access another emotional level. He says of himself
that he is malicious and manipulative.*

*At sessions, sometimes he becomes "feminine", sometimes "masculine",
sometimes dark. He says he is better off when people refer to him using feminine
or neuter pronouns. His name in the neutral is Max. I accept his desire by post-
poning that the search for one's own identity is a path on which, depending on
the moment, the words with which we identify ourselves can change. I recognize
that, at this moment, it is the way he "feels most comfortable" and session is a
space where it's good to be comfortable. I apologize in advance if I am wrong
and, when it happens, we reflect precisely on how much neutrality has to do with
the potential to be many things rather than "being nothing". In this vein, we will
end up using, randomly, masculine, feminine, and neutral pronouns (in cases
where the Italian language allows it).*

The first images with which, consequently, we can be, are the pawns, the puppets of
our game: the *Player Characters (PC)* in the sense of "fictional characters *controlled*
or *controllable* by the player". PCs execute user commands, like maneuverable virtual puppets, necessary for gamers to interact with the game world. They are models
with which to identify oneself temporarily in order to carry out otherwise unattain-
able actions of which they do not seem to be aware. On a symbolic level, I would
consider them to be like the puppets of the sandbox, with which the patient plays to
represent a scene. To help me visualize them, I usually rely on the terminology used
in role-playing games to describe *ethical alignment* (*Good, Neutral, Evil*) or the *way
to adhere to game rules* (*Chaotic, Neutral, Lawful*).

*I ask him if he has any passions. M., at first, tells me that since being sick he
has had no interest in anything, but the last anime that had fascinated him was
Clash of the Titans, especially the protagonist of the saga, Eren Jaeger. Speaking of passions, he tells me that he loves horror movies, especially Dario Ar-
gento's ones and cinema in general but, since the lockdown, he has lost interest
in that too. He reports that he does not like them for the impressive scenes of
violence, but for the story behind it and how they tell it ("they are rhetorical figures that send meanings", he says). I ask him to give me an example and he talks
to me about the Joker. In these first months of therapy, under my encouragement,
he manages to see a movie again and to resume playing his Play Station, specifically Zelda – The Adventures of Link.*

1.3. Imagine Behaviors also as Adventures to Be Overcome

Often, at first, in the narratives of the episodes of acting out, the images are not
accompanied by psychic emotions or feelings: they are devoid of creativity, like a
stereotype, a mimicry, revealing a great amount of *titanism*.[3] Living the dramatic

reality of the episodes in the moment of the session, imagining these actions, in parallel, as *adventures* or *missions*, allows us to rely on the imagination in the search for creative solutions, managing to support the emotional load. Now, let's try to read M.'s stories having in the background the characteristics of the PCs that emerged from the descriptions of his "passions", without saturating or literalizing: they seem to see a hero in distress, struggling with terrifying monsters who, desperate, fail to make sense of his attempts.

> *M. describes himself almost exclusively through the violence of his self-cutting acts, of his first dreams: images of getting hurt, hurting others, parents first of all, with a knife, which seem to cover everything.*
>
> *Four months into therapy, Max begins hanging out with a group of school kids; he starts dabbling with pills and drugs until he is hospitalized for taking seven Xanax and, at the same time, is taken over by the territorial psychiatric service for adolescents as an emergency (June 2021).*

As in the case of M., often adolescents, on the one hand, would like to be seen, to say something about themselves but, for fear of "being eaten", they can build a very intricate labyrinth around themselves. And behind, to operate the PCs, there is almost always a child, scared and angry.

2.   Phase II: Imagining PCs as Parts of Self: Dramatis Personae

> *After hospitalization, with the taking over by the territorial psychiatric service of competence, the relationship with the first private psychiatrist is interrupted. She resumes hanging out with a group of peers and makes virtual friendships on Dischord; moreover, for some months now, she has entered into a relationship with a boy from another region, met online. After hospitalization, his mother hides the drugs from him, but M. candidly admits that when he is with her friends, he happened to be taking benzodiazepines for recreational purposes.*

2.1.   Look for the Masks

As we have seen so far, the renunciation of conceptual thought and the listening-observation disposition of the relational game, therefore, allow access to that state of *reverie*, to that place of meditation between dream and wakefulness, so that the analyst can propose to understand something completely new and unknown. Very often adolescents, on the other hand, ask us to give a name to their experiences and behaviors that most disturb them. It is important, however, not to give in to the temptation to saturate the meanings with alternative definitions, which would arrive as extraneous to the patient, not felt by him but imposed. Rather, the young patient must be given the freedom to be able to be many things, passing from "one mask to another", according to the situation and the emotion of the moment;

being able to stay in *fluidity*, in indefinition, gradually putting a bridge between his behavior and his emotions.

The internal chaos emerges loud and clear from his speeches, in his desperate attempt to define himself: "Am I depressed or obsessive? Olanzapine is an antipsychotic, so I'm also psychotic? And what does it mean?" Speaking of "defining herself" (or being defined), I ask her how her "identity" search is progressing, if she still recognizes herself in the non-binary label. She tells me that now she recognizes herself as Demi-girl: that is, she partially identifies with the female universe. He reports that his mother continues to pursue and insult him; he is overwhelmed by it, alternating experiences of hatred with experiences of guilt. He feels great anxiety and internal chaos, he is frightened, every now and then he bursts into uncontrollable laughter and in the evening, when he finds himself in his room, he has "bad thoughts". At least he doesn't cut himself anymore, reporting that he no longer feels the same need.

2.2. Between Representing to Conceal and Representing to Show

Often the behaviors of adolescents are, in the eyes of adults, incomprehensible, inexplicable. This is because, in moments of crisis, they can be used as attempts both to hide or remove an internal experience that is too frightening and to represent and communicate to others something that is happening on a deeper level. And it will be in the space *between* these two polarities that the encounter with the internal characters (*Dramatis Personae*) will take place. These masks, in fact, play a part in the simulated representation of the session, animating it, giving voice to the patient's emotions and moods. Like the masks of the theater that, *coming on stage*,[4] transform stories into *dramatis scenae*, encouraging us to follow Hermes along that ridge between *representing to conceal* and *representing to show*. In this way the actions are designed and aimed to produce some form of interior transformation, enhancing gestures and rituals in the context of reciprocity; a poetic making, which allows an experiential adventure capable of favoring a process of digestion of events.[5]

Shortly before the summer break, M. resumes his social life, appreciating, even if with difficulty, the time shared with others. During one of our sessions, she accidentally makes a noisy burp; embarrassed, she apologizes, but she laughs out loud at the gaffe and, on several occasions, she remembers it with amusement. I ask him if she has plans for the summer. She will go on vacation with her parents, but she doesn't really want to, especially because she is ashamed to show her male body in a bathing suit and the scars due to cuts. She also tells me that she is playing a new mobile game: Genshin Impact, describing it as a "more modern Zelda, where there are many characters to be found". About this, to facilitate her in describing the confused amalgam of ambivalent emotions that inhabited her at that time, I ask her which were "her" (internal) characters. She tells me it's like she has three moods.

Moved by these suggestions, I tried to imagine, right through an attitude of *active imaginal play*, some passages of the last sessions before the summer break, as lines of a theatrical scene between the various *masks* or *moods*, to use the patient's expression. The result is a multi-part monologue, with *nonsense* tones that bring to mind Beckett's theater; a dramatic representation of the, sometimes insurmountable, difficulty of M. to put boundaries between itself and the other.

To follow, then, the description of this Imaginal Active Play, in the form of a *theatrical script*, in which I come on stage as well, as the Therapist.

DRAMATIS PERSONAE
Characters/Moods
GENNY [pain in the ass, she just gets pissed off]
DEPRESSED MAX
MANIAC MAX [manages to banish thoughts but it's not so normal]
THE THERAPIST [*myself*]
Act I

DEPRESSED MAX	When my parents yell at me, I feel like I'm being fired with a bullet the size of my whole body.
GENNY	When I was little, my mother would get angry if I hurt myself.
DEPRESSED MAX	It is as if everything were embodied by me.
MANIAC MAX	My mind does what it wants! [*laughs*]
DEPRESSED MAX	As if I were empty, I feel nothing.
GENNY	Massimo has been gone for 2 years, everything has collapsed.
MANIAC MAX	It's nice to have fun with people! [*burps*]
THE THERAPIST	*We say goodbye for the holidays, a review of these first months of therapy?*
DEPRESSED MAX	At first it was like I was inside a giant bubble, in the dark . . .
GENNY	. . . I couldn't free myself.
MANIAC MAX	Starting to go out again and going back to school . . .
GENNY	. . . The bubble has burst!
DEPRESSED MAX	Only that I was inside another bubble . . .
GENNY	Bigger . . .
MANIAC MAX	But illuminated!

2.3. Appreciate the Reciprocity of Playing Together

By listening to what the masks have to tell, we create the necessary conditions so that the patient can rely on us, feeling seen in the many aspects of him. Above all, he will be able to feel that the analyst has recognized his *desire*, and he allows him to express it in its playful aspects, showing him the power of loving and oriented thought. In this phase, it can appear in the session, in the form of an image (or scene or story), an element of novelty, of rebirth, of potentiality, which resonates with the emotional experience of the events shared so far, external and internal to the session.

> *M.'s family decides to take a cat and entrust its care to him, thinking, albeit with little conviction, that it could help him get better. M. seems to invest a lot in the cat (as, despite the fatigue, in therapy) and when he talks to me about it he says: "It was love at first sight. Of course, it's a responsibility but if you educate him well from an early age he doesn't make a mess."*
>
> *Furthermore, the choice of the cat's name does not seem casual: the family decides to call him W., but in reality M. would have wanted to call him Eevee, the neutral pokemon, the only one to have more alternatives of evolution, depending on the magical power to which it is exposed.*

3.   Phase III: Enter the Game

> *Upon returning to work, after the summer break (September 2021), M. immediately demonstrates a certain difficulty in resuming therapy and he forgets to come to the first session. Despite her fatigue, in September, she begins to go back to school; during that same period her psychiatrist is forced to take a leave of absence for personal reasons.*
>
> *M.'s confusion and fear increase when, due to a series of bureaucratic difficulties, the substitute for the colleague is late in arriving and four different psychiatrists see him, adding more chaos to him. One of them, after having examined him, tells me that my patient feels very bad, suggesting that I should have seen him more times a week. He changes his drug therapy; the following days M. does not go to school and skips the session with me because he sleeps all day. The mother tells me that M. is angry and he'd like to suspend every kind of therapy.*

3.1.   Actively Participate in Transference/Countertransference Emotions

Sometimes, in the most critical situations, having in mind and sharing the metaphor of the game may not be enough. In fact, the tendency of psychosis to concretize symbolic reality often makes it difficult to access deeper levels. When the chaos around increases, on the other hand, it emphasizes the need to remain anchored to something tangible, corporeal. For this reason, our clinical interventions will have to pass through actions, gestures, transforming the concreteness of the patient's actions first within us, listening to the transference and countertransference movements, then re-proposing them to him in the form of symbolic acts (*talking acts*).

> *The latest events arouse a strong emotion within me, activating a protective maternal instinct and I tell M, via message, that I understand "and feel" his anger*

and that I can help him. He manages to return to the session and bring his fear: "It's all too real. I feel without goals or interests." The Black Bubble becomes a "Black Hole, which has so much energy that it absorbs everything and there is no way out".

Life seems like a game I don't know how to play."

3.2. Playing Together

It is important and often necessary, at this point, to do something *with* the patient, which is creative, expressive, stimulating, and symbolically meaningful. In this specific case I use a board game, but it could also be an artistic work, a piece of writing, whatever we feel could have value in that precise moment of therapy. The constructive act of *playing together* (in the broadest sense of the term) constitues an intermediate expressive space, neither purely internal nor purely external, where differences and equality are equally tolerable.

Since he talked about games, I ask him if he plays or has ever played board games. He tells me no, that he would have liked it, but his parents didn't like it. I ask him if he wants to play a game with me and he agrees.

Before playing with M., I have to be welcomed "in his room" and I ask him to describe it: he tells me the arrangement of the furniture, dirty clothes everywhere, the bed, the window with the LEDs around it. The next session, therefore, I try to put some magic in M.'s "chaotic game", bringing "The Magic Labyrinth".

Each of the players must take some treasures in this labyrinth; at each turn, new roads open up and you have to be careful not to close them. In this game the paths are mobile, it is up to each participant to create the way to the treasure by putting up or removing walls; if desired, everything can also return as before. Max enters the game, immediately understands the rules, adapts the strategy to the changes, takes one treasure after another, but his emotionality is inhibited. When our time ends, I just point out to him that he, sometimes, had made moves that had closed his paths and possibilities.

3.3. Bringing the Gaming Experience Back to
   Listening in the Session

After having had a concrete experience, in the game, it will be more easily tolerable to be with both *emptiness* and *excess*, with *fluidity* and *rigidity*, participating together in the dialectical process.

In the following sessions, we manage to stay together in M.'s labyrinth of emotions, constantly changing direction, according to the obstacles we encounter: a Sadness that leads to Hatred, as when his friends do not look for him; nonsense can trigger hatred that is already inside her, she says, and arguments with the

Dischord's users make hate more like a strange liberating euphoria ("when I argue I feel free"). Since we were going through the various facets of anger and hatred, I point out to him how often he used this word, even for very different situations and people. I propose to him, at home, in sessions or in class, when he was bored not following the lesson, to draw up a "Hate Chart" which we would then comment on together. At the forefront there is always her entire "homophobic" family, especially her mother, who continues to believe that depression is just an excuse for not going to school. It was not the first time that someone had said something like this to him (doctors, teachers, classmates) and we wonder why: maybe that "sadness that becomes anger towards others" can poison us to the point of intoxicating our relationships? What to do with that anger to prevent it from transforming again, taking the path of malignity?

3.4. Imagine a Bridge with the Collective Unconscious

Like active imagination, playing also allows us to create a bridge, a dialogue, between the personal unconscious and the collective unconscious. The *cultural* and *social* function of the game allows you to get back in touch with archetypal images, to establish connections with others, exchanging symbols and creating new ones.

In those sessions, his lazy passive destructiveness triggered in me, in a compensatory way, a passionate rage: I was reminded of the battles of the LGBTQ+ community to have their civil rights recognized; the anger and frustration for the marginalization and humiliations suffered, transformed into a vital energy of change, which has nourished and continues to fuel his activism, with a great spirit of acceptance and openness towards the other. Of all this M. knew nothing, hardly knew the Pride. Perhaps before hating, it was important to study and learn about things and history. For this reason, I invite him to deepen the subject and to get information, encouraging him to commit himself so that others, in the future, do not suffer the suffering and discrimination that he himself has experienced on many occasions, at school as well as in family life. All these talks lead her to recognize how much the idea of getting better scares her, precisely because it would involve an opening towards the world for which she does not yet feel ready. She just wants to be left, at home, with her cat.

Attention to images and relationships with the Other (and the collective), playing together, following him in the labyrinth, can facilitate, in the young patient, a reconstruction and reassembling, putting together what is missing, provoking an activation emotional and, finally, giving voice to that memory (calling it, getting in touch with it). Being able to share these deep emotions, freely, in the space of the session, gives the patient the possibility, on a relational level, to trust and invest in the relationship with the Other. The image of the *embryonic self* (the cat Eevee in

M.'s case) will gradually go through further *evolutions*: it will become our *compass*, which, by showing us where we are, also reveals where we are going, helping us to understand where we want to go.

> *In the following sessions M. seems to go through a depressive phase but, as he himself admits, he is "more aware", which leads to self-reflection. Some images of the hospitalization (gastric lavage, sedation, drips) come to mind; sadness, anger, fear, bewilderment appear. He cries, something melts: the emotions seem to come out in an authentic way. After so much wandering, overcoming walls and curves, at the end of the labyrinth, we have found a first treasure of authenticity.*
>
> *Finally, he tells me about the latest developments in the relationship with the cat: initially he thought he hated her because she did not purr, but they gradually got to know each other by playing together. In the last sessions of the year, he brings, with sweet and affectionate tones, the image of the "soft and perfumed" cat after grooming itself, which finally purrs: "Before he was suspicious because he missed his mother. Now I don't force her to stay with me. But he still doesn't make the dough [knead his paws] on me."*

4.   Phase IV: The Avatars

> *Towards the end of 2021, just before the Christmas break, her mother, disappointed by the public service, insists that M. go to another private psychiatrist. M. does not want to, she understandably refuses to see another doctor; for this reason, she tells me, she has argued with both parents and hasn't spoken to her father since ("they can't empathize with my pain", she says). She feels pressed and reverses day for night. Meanwhile M. is assigned a new psychiatrist, who will replace the colleague on leave and will follow him permanently.*
>
> *With the beginning of the new year and with the resumption of sessions, M. returns to school and resumes going out with her best friend. She goes back to the movie theater and tells me that, at that time, she had seen some horror movies and she tells me about them.*

4.1.   Beyond the Mask

Having been able to "peek" behind the mask, it is important for the patient to experiment with other ways of using his masks, questioning them. In this way it will be more natural to approach the complex/archetypal nuclei of those hidden/represented fragilities.

> *The stable assignment of a psychiatrist seems to provide some order to M., but she starts this new relationship with little confidence; in session she says that she wants to convince the new psychiatrist to do what she says ("I have to do things my way," she comments). We work on the difficulty of trusting people and*

the use we make of our masks/moods: when do they help us? When, on the other hand, do they hinder us?

4.2. Confrontation with the Images (Avatars)

Arriving at this stage of therapy, the new images/characters/masks that emerge seem to take on the *Avatar* valences, signaling a further transformation. The term *avatar*, in modern computer language, indicates the *image chosen from users to represent themselves in a virtual community*. The word derives from the Sanskrit *avatāra*, lit. *descended, passed through*. In the Hindu cult of Vishnu the *avatar* is one of the physical forms assumed by the god when he descends to Earth to restore the Cosmic Order (*Dharma*) and summarize the differences in a stable religious manifestation.

These images, this time, reveal to us the possibility of the coexistence of affective polarities of opposite signs, reacting to the events of the external world also according to them (the mask that looks both inside and outside): unconscious identities that originate from the collective unconscious. The presentation of these *unconscious identities*, *descended* into the "other world" of the session, allows the patient to access the emotions behind the mask, dialogue and confront with them, inserting them into his own stories.

> *He tells me that he has reviewed the remake of* Scream*; it made him think about hospitalization, because, in those days, they had shown its parody,* Scary Movie*, a film that, instead, he found hilarious. Thinking back to that period she talks to me about the scars, she realizes, scared and disgusted, how evident and deep they are. She says she has also reviewed some classics, including* Suspiria*, by Dario Argento, one of her favorite movies, and she's surprised at how creepy and distressing it can be; she even wonders how she could be not afraid of this kind of movie. At home the situation remains mostly unchanged, especially the non-dialogue with her father situation; her mother, on the other hand, from Christmas onwards, confides more in her sister and seems to be helping her to better understand the pain of M., who feels less pressured ("she seems changed", she comments). At the end of a session, he expresses, with dreamy eyes, his impatience and enthusiasm for the imminent release of new Genshin characters and shows me some of them. I ask her which, of the many collected, is her favorite character ever, the one in which she most recognizes herself; she immediately replies: "Ayaka, a magical princess who uses the power of ice; she has a fan and an ice sword. Even my friend A. says I remember her a lot."*

4.3. Complexual Nuclei and Archetypal Resonances

Let's see how these images are enriched with shades of deep meanings, when they emerge within a narrative in which, in the here and now of the session, the actualized memory of what has already been manages to stay together with the thought of what could be. Being able to imagine oneself, projected into the future, opens up the *desire* and trust towards the other and the world, necessary to grow up and express one's potential. Putting aside the more rigid symptoms and masks, we can now face the archetypal fear of growth and change; the ghost of verification, performance, competition with others.

> *Once the updates are over, I ask him about his plans for this year and for his future in general. At first he replies that he cannot see himself in the future. He surely wants to start the transition process ("I can't be male"), but he is afraid to tell his parents, fearing their reaction. I tell her that I understand his fears and remind her that she is not alone, that both her psychiatrist and I could have accompanied her and helped to communicate it to her parents. He does not respond, but something unlocks, he starts talking about the future again: "I wouldn't like to grow up, I'd like to have a little more time to feel better and live my adolescence . . . I'd like to feel fear." He recognizes that if the transition does not begin soon, it's difficult to see herself in the future. If he tries to imagine post-transition life, the only "project" is becoming a stripper and she giggles as she says it. I tell her that the future may be full of possibilities, even more so it would be better to finish school. About this he says that he too would like to finish (because "it sucks") but, at the same time, he would not want to study. Smiling, I tell her it would be nice, but it's a bit difficult . . . She tells me that, in fact, now she would like to do well in school, get to the final year ballots with the highest average to be able to get promoted without taking the final exam.*

At the same time, it will be possible to experience the desire for growth, for enrichment that only the presence and knowledge of the other are able to provide.

> *In that period, moreover, she brings me a great event that she will talk about at length: finally the cat has "made the dough" on her. She tells me that she loves him very much and is very fond of him. She sometimes fears that the cleaning lady might leave the windows open and the cat might jump down and run away or get hurt. Once she even dreamed about it and she got very scared.*

This is because it was possible to experience reality from a sensory and, at the same time, imaginative point of view, till producing an *aesthetic response*.[6] With this expression we mean the possibility of welcoming the world inside, holding our breath in wonder, letting ourself be amazed by its beauty, feeling the availability of each event to be the object of imagination, its presence as a *psychic reality*.[7] Therefore, there is the sensation of a first *symbolic synthesis* of the images that have emerged so far, the product of the shared therapeutic path. For all these reasons, in this phase, it may be useful to amplify the images that have emerged, up to the archetypal level, to know their stratifications of meanings. I would like to clarify that these amplifications are useful above all to us, to continue working with the patient while remaining in contact with the collective and archetypal plan, how much and whether sharing with him will be up to the sensitivity of the therapist, to his internal setting, to the characteristics of that therapeutic relationship, of that *shared game*. Staying always on the edge between the individual and the collective.

Ghostface, the serial killer of the Scream *saga, takes his name from the mask he wears, whose shape brings to mind Munch's painting "The Scream". Usually, before attacking his victims with a knife, he entertains them on the phone with various questions, usually related to horror movies. His talent lies in playing with suspense but, above all, in having a particular speed in disappearing in the rare moments of difficulty, almost to seem like a real ghost. Even if, over the course of numerous films, the serial killer is invariably a different character, the mask always has the same shape. Behind it is always a person possessed by the ghost of Rancor, of Revenge, of Sadism; a sort of dark collective projection of the great archetypal emotions (fear, anger, disappointment), which from catharsis degenerates into psychotic inflation when someone wears it, becoming possessed by it.*

In Scary Movie, *on the contrary, the "serial killer" sings rap, smokes marijuana, and the phone calls to his victims often end in hilarious ways. The peculiarity of this mask (despite the shape being almost the same as the original) is in the changing facial expressions depending on the situation and emotion of the moment. The "killer", in this case, is unable to scare or eliminate victims in the ways he would like, and only manages to kill by mistake and in surreal ways. This time the mask seems to place itself between the Self and the World, managing to look both inside and outside, like the most significant masks of the Nō theater, which manage to "change expression" depending on light, capturing both the essential and fixed nature of the emotion as the changing nature of the emotional life.*

Kamisato Ayaka, the playable character of Genshin, is the eldest daughter of the Kamisato clan and is seen by everyone as a model of perfection. She is a kindhearted girl with a pleasant temperament and treats others with kindness and courtesy. She cares about the inhabitants of her city and goes out of her way to help them when they are in trouble. Everyone admires her. For these reasons she was awarded the honorary title of Shirasagi Himegimi ("Princess frost heron"): the elegance and bearing of a princess, the mastery in the art of the sword of a skilled warrior and the spiritual strength of an ice witch, "graceful as snow in the wind, elegant as a heron perched in the courtyard". In Egyptian mythology the heron is a symbol of rebirth and transformation; in the Book of the Dead the Shenty heron, with its solunar characteristics, represents a bridge between the Worlds. Every year, in the period of the floods, Shenty returned to the Nile heralding the newfound fertility and abundance such as the beginning of a new cycle. He was represented in some tombs, adored by the deceased, as a symbol of rebirth and transformation. The Greek legend of Phoenix originates from this myth. In India, on the other hand, for its disturbing gaze and its ag-gressive behavior towards smaller animals, it represents isolation, quarrels and a lack of scruples.

5. Conclusions: The Dashavatara

The Dashavatara (from the Sanskrit *daśāvatāra*), in Hinduism, represents the ten (*daśa*) main incarnations (*avatāra*) of Vishnu, the times when he descended to Earth to restore the cosmic order. Although the order and list of avatars changes between sects and regions, the ones that come back most in many versions are the following:

1 *Matsya*: the *fish* avatar, who announces the imminent destruction of the world by means of fires and floods to King Vaivasvata Manu.
2 *Kurma*: the *giant tortoise* avatar, which supports Mount Mandara in the myth of the "blending of the cosmic milk Ocean" (*Samutramanthan*).
3 *Varah*: the *giant boar* avatar who, after a battle lasting a thousand years against the evil Hiranyaksha, brings the Earth out of the cosmic Ocean between its fangs and places it back in its place in the universe.
4 *Narasimha*: the *half man/half lion* avatar, who puts an end to the religious per-secutions perpetrated by Hiranyakashipu by gutting him with his claws.
5 *Vamana*: the *dwarf* avatar, who manages to restore sovereignty over the Three Kingdoms (Heaven, Earth, and the Underworld) to the gods, reconquering them, to the king of the asuras Bali, becoming a giant and taking three steps.
6 *Parashurama*: the *warrior armed with axe* avatar, who repeatedly defeats the kṣatriyas (a caste of arrogant warriors), who oppressed the priestly caste of the Brahmans, restoring their legitimate supremacy.
7 *Rama*: the *common prince without powers* avatar, which symbolizes Morality and the Rule, who defeats the evil demon Rāvana, saving the princess kid-napped by him.
8 *Krishna*: embodies the *supreme God* and represents divine love for the human soul.
9 *Buddah*: *enlightened man*, who preaches the way of ahimsa (non-violence).
10 *Kalki*: the *last incarnation* of Vishnu, who appears to end the *Kali Yuga*, the final cycle of an era, when only chaos, evil, and persecution prevail and the Dharma has vanished. He will arrive riding a white horse and his sword will be unsheathed, burning like a comet, to restart another cycle of existence.

Some modern interpretations see the ten main avatars of Vishnu as an ascend-ing order from simple life forms (such as fish, amphibians, mammals) to more complex life forms (human, heroic, enlightened and divine forms) and see the Dashavatara as a reflection, or a foreshadowing, of the modern theory of evolu-tion. Another reading, however, considers it as a *parable of evolution* that does not approve of evolutionism, but alludes to transformative phases of spiritual progress through infinite cycles of creationism. For some it is wrong to give an evolutionary reading to avatars, above all because it risks degrading the divine status of Rama and Krishna in comparison with the Buddha's: they are all supremely divine and perfect, each for the *circumstances in which they appeared.*

Regardless of what the "exact" meaning of Vishnu's avatars is, taking into account what has been said so far, I believe it is necessary to consider the contemporary presence of several levels of meanings, which coexist, more or less stratified in the collective Unconscious, influencing its representations and traditions. From a Jungian point of view, it could be said that it is precisely the very high spiritual complexity of Hinduism that does not distance it from science (as opposed to other religions), allowing it to welcome it as another manifestation of man; therefore, in some way, divine.

Even in the therapy game, it is possible to find, in the imaginal production, an evolutionary trend, from *simple* forms (archaic, polarized, rigid) to more *complex* and personal forms, emotionally connoted, resulting from relationships with the others, up to the emerging underlying archetypal meanings. At the same time, however, we realize that these meanings were already present behind all the images and were waiting for the necessary conditions to *manifest* themselves, the *right* moment, revealing their coexistence, *circular*, along *infinite cycles of destruction and creation.* The game frame lays the foundations for all of this to happen.

Regarding this, the invitation of James Hillman will be a fundamental mantra when we explore mental labyrinths of young adults:

> We have to go back to the ancient mind, to be able to see the figure behind the tiles of the visible. Because each image holds together the formidable complexity of the multiple and is therefore a mosaic.[8]

During the adolescent period, each *avatar* can be used, depending on the moment, as a *PC* or as a *dramatis persona* and, within and through the *game* setting, the adolescent will be able to experience their *deep archetypal potential*, when the soul will begin to produce figures and fantasies born from the imagination of the heart. It will be up to the therapist to recognize the connections between mythological images and emotional facts/conflicts, for the patient's sake. The *active Imaginal play attitude* helped me to stay on the limit (*sub-limen*) between *letting the unconscious happen* and *allowing it to express itself.* The metaphor of *Dashavatara* can be a useful reference image to accompany the young adult, not only in his *Hero's Journey* of development and structuring of an egoic consciousness (absolutely fundamental and *necessary* for the identity process), but also in its *cycles of spiritual (co)creation*, staying in the *chaos* that necessarily precedes them. And these avatars will be both representations of present models, both syntheses of past images, and projections of future potential.

Inspired by all these images, I wanted to represent the ten avatars of M. as a multiplicity of Parts of the emerging Self, seeking a dialogue between them; complexes, more or less autonomous, satellites of a central conscious-ness in fieri. Consequently, the "order" I propose for the appearance of M.'s avatars (which will frame my final considerations on the case) must be understood as just one of the many readings that could be done. Depending on the obstacles and curves that we will encounter, in the labyrinth of the emo-tions of therapy, it will be up to us to rely on images to find and take one of the many possible paths.

MAX'S DASHAVATARA

1 *Eeren Jaeger* (*Clash of the Titans*) (Chaotic Good). The wounded child, con-fused between the *human* and the *titanic*; witnessed helplessly the "universal deluge" (*Attack of the Giants*), which led to the destruction of the previous order and the death of the family (*puberty*, the chaos of adolescence that trans-forms and polarizes the relationship between hatred and love).

2 *Joker* (Chaotic Evil). A *Shadowy* figure, alone *carrying* the weight of his pain on his shoulders; the anger and depression unheeded by the family and society which risks degenerating into *envy* and *wickedness*.

3 *Link* (Lawful Good). The *heroic child*, who tries to free his Anima figure by solving puzzles and labyrinths; the omnipotent hope of the *Puer* to be able to *restore the previous order*, ignoring the need for change.

4 *Giusy* (angry mood). The defensive *Persona*, who pushes and attacks others with his *claws*.

5 *Depressed Max* (depressed mood). The depressive mask, which suffers from loneliness and feels misunderstood, sucked into the black hole from which he cannot escape. He can be *small*, stand in the background, or become *gigantic*, until covering everything.

6 *Maniac Max* (euphoric mood). The character of extroversion, which is acti-vated when M. is with his friends; he is unpredictable, he likes to be in com-pany but he does strange things, burps and laughs for no reason. He banishes depression when it's too *overwhelming*.

7 *Ghostface* (*Scream*) (Neutral Evil). The symbol of Hatred and Resentment, but also the *demon* of depression, who wanders like a ghost from the past, ready to *kidnap* the vital parts. Like a cursed tribal mask, if worn, it can lead to the suspension of *rules* and *moral order*.

8 *Scaryface* (*Scary Movie*) (Chaotic Neutral). The way out from depressive clo-sure: the opening towards the other and the world that leads to *love towards human beings*; from the disquieting fixity of anguish to the possibility of *changing expression* (after having faced the *ghosts* of the past, as if to make them a "parody").

9 *Kamisato Ayaka* (*Genshin Impact*) (Lawful Good). The *wise* and *enlightened* ice heron princess, a symbol of hope for the future and rebirth (even if, on the one hand, she would like to "freeze time" and not have to think about the future).

10 *Eevee* (*Cat*) (Neutral Neutral). The cat *W./Eevee*, which has yet to *manifest* and define itself, a symbol of relational and affective investment. Precious product of the therapeutic process still in progress, delicate, in need of care, attention, respect, welcoming both its *wild* and *domestic* nature.

In conclusion, the attitude of *active imaginal play* allows us to stay with the behaviors of PCs, finding meaning in acting-outs, seeing and listening to the *masks* they wear (the emotions behind the behaviors). Through *playing together*, it becomes possible to stay in the relationship, in the patient's affective labyrinth without being destroyed by it. Playing, as repeatedly stated, takes on more than just a containing function, as if certain things can be said, done, felt only by playing together, in a protected place, with shared rules. In that space it does not try to fill the void or to give a name to things, but it has the new feeling that something can come out from the self and can be tolerated and understood. All this favors that passage from the *dramatic representation* to the *emotional expression*, up to the *ethical confront*, with the images of the past, the present, and the future in the form of *avatars* that are further enriched, in resonance with all the others, of archetypal nuances.

> *Today, M., while going through the usual fluctuations, speaks, in an increasingly aware way, of transition and the need to tell the parents, to begin the process as soon as possible: "I can't stand the idea of having to face puberty and see myself as a male." For this reason, he is considering the possibility of getting help, from me and/or from his psychiatrist, to communicate his wishes to his parents, in a protected setting. She recognizes herself in the definition "transexual woman". So what Hillman says is true. Finding the right word can be magnificent; words are like pillows: if well arranged they relieve pain.*[9]

Playing, through the imagination, with myths and archetypal images, means dealing with very precise models of the mechanisms of the human mind, drawing real *maps of psyche*. This is because the ego individualizes itself, becomes unique, in becoming more objective and universal. To conclude, quoting Bernhard: "What is most intimate, most subjective, what touches the depths of a human being the most, his most secret drama, is also what is most universal, what touches everyone."[10]

Notes

1 P. Fonagy, M. Target, "*Playing with reality,* vol. I: *Theory of mind and the normal development of psychic reality*", pp. 679–700.
2 C.G. Jung. "Medicina e psicoterapia", *Opere*, vol. 16.
3 R. Lopez Pedraza. "*Sul Titanismo. Un incontro tra la patologia e la poesia*".
4 M.L. Von Franz, "*L'immaginazione attiva*".
5 J. Hillman, "*Le storie che curano*".
6 J. Hillman, "*Politica della bellezza*", Chapter IV, *La pratica della bellezza*, pp. 94–97.

7 J. Hillman, S. Ronchey, "*L'ultima immagine*", Introduzione, *Paganesimo*, p. 16.
8 J. Hillman, S. Ronchey, "*L'ultima immagine*", Introduzione, *Imago vera*, p. 23.
9 J. Hillman, S. Ronchey, "*L'ultima immagine*", *Restare Pensante*, p. 38.
10 E. Bernhard, "*Mitobiografia*", *Introduzione*, p. XXXIX.

References

Adler G. (1966). *Studies in Analytical Psychology*, London: Hodder & Stoughton.

Bernhard E. (1969). *Mitobiografia*, ed. H. Erba-Tissot, trans. G. Bemporad, 7th ed., Milan: Biblioteca Adelphi.

Fonagy P., Target M. (1996). "Playing with reality, vol. I: Theory of mind and the normal development of psychic reality", *International Journal of Psychoanalysis*, 77, pp. 679–700; Italian version, "*Giocare con la realtà*, vol. I: *Teoria della mente e sviluppo normale nella realtà psichica*", in Fonagy and Target (2001, 29–56).

Hillman J. (1983). *Le storie che curano*, Milan: Raffaello Cortina.

Hillman J. (1999). *Politica della bellezza*, ed. Francesco Donfrancesco, trans. Paola Donfrancesco, Bergamo: Moretti & Vitali.

Hillman J., Ronchey S. (2021). *L'ultima immagine*, Milan: Rizzoli – Mondadori.

Jung C.G. (1945). "Medicina e psicoterapia", *Opere*, 16.

Lopez Pedraza, R. (1987). "Sul Titanismo. Un incontro tra la patologia e la poesia", trans. and ed. Maria Rosaria Buri and Michele Pesante, in *L'Immaginale. Rassegna di psicologia immaginale*, V, April 1987.

Von Franz, M.L. (1978). "L'immaginazione attiva", *Rivista di Psicologia Analitica*, 17.

Further Reading

ARAS (Archive for Research in Archetypal Symbolism) (2011). *Il Libro dei Simboli. Riflessioni sulle Immagini Archetipiche*, Italian edn. eds. Crimi, S. and Frigo, A., trans. Rebecchi, C., Satta, P., Valdettaro, M., Modena: Taschen.

Baricco, A. (2018). *The Game*, Turin: Giulio Einaudi editore s.p.a.

Bosio, W. (2022). "Immagini e processo analitico" in *Sandplay e psicopatologie gravi*, eds. Pattis Zoja, E. and Castellana, F., Bergamo: Moretti and Vitali.

Correale, A. (2006). *Area traumatica e campo istituzionale*, Rome: Edizioni Borla.

Cortese, M. (2009). "Prassi terapeutiche junghiane in un servizio di salute mentale", *Rivista di Psicologia Analitica*, 79(27).

Croci, A. (1998). "Il gioco simbolico nell'intervallo tra il balocco e il mondo" in *Temenos junghiano*.

Demetrio, D. (1997). *Il gioco della vita. Kit autobiografico. Trenta proposte per il piacere di raccontarsi*, Milan: Guerini e Associati.

Di Cesare, G. (2009). "La riabilitazione psichiatrica tra Metis ed Hermes", *Rivista di Psicologia Analitica*, 79(27).

Diatkine, R. (1972). "*L'apporto della teoria psicoanalitica alla comprensione dei malati mentali e, eventualmente, all'organizzazione delle istituzioni destinate a curarli*" in *Lo psicoanalista senza divano. La psicoanalisi e le strutture psichiatriche*, trans. from the original, Racamier, P.C., *Le Psychanalyste sans divan* (ed. Payot, Parigi) di Vera Varalda, Milan: Raffaello Cortina Editore (1982).

Ferretti, G. (2013). *"Gli aironi"* in *L'Officina dell'Ambiente* (February 2013).

Fordham, M. (1956). "Active Imagination and Imaginative Activity", *Journal of Analytical Psychology*, vol. I.

Hillman, J. (1972). *Saggio su Pan*, Milan: Raffaello Cortina (1977).

Hillman, J. (1975). *Re-visione della psicologia*, Italian trans., Milan: Adelphi, 1992, 2019 ("The Adelphi").

Huizinga, J. (1938). *"Homo ludens. Proeve eener bepaling van het spel-element der cultuur"*, Italian edn. *"Homo ludens"*, trans. and ed. Corinna von Schendel, Milan: Il Saggiatore (1967).

Jung, C.G. (1917/1943). "Psicologia dell'Inconscio", *Opere*, vol. VII, Turin: Boringhieri (1983).

Jung, C.G. (1935). *"Principi di psicoterapia pratica"*, *Opere*, vol. 16, Turin: Bollati Boringhieri.

Jung, C.G. (1978). *Ricordi, sogni, riflessioni*, Milan: Bur, Rizzoli.

Jung, C.G. (2009). *Il Libro Rosso: Liber Novus. Edizione studio*, ed. Shamdasani, S., trans. from the original, *The Red Book: Liber Novus. A Reader's edition*, eds. Sorge G., Massimello M. A., Schiavoni G., Giannachi, L.M. (The Foundation of C.G. Jung, Zurigo), Turin: Bollati Boringhieri.

Lingiardi, V. (2001). *L'alleanza terapeutica*, Milan: Raffaello Cortina Editore.

Mackenzie Brown, C. (2010). "Vivekananda and the scientific legitimation of Advaita Vedanta". In James R. Lewis; Olav Hammer (eds.), *Handbook of Religion and the Authority of Science*. Leiden: BRILL, p. 227.

Mackenzie Brown, C. (2012). *Hindu Perspectives on Evolution: Darwin, Dharma, and Design*. London and New York: Routledge, pp. 163–164.

Maffei, G. (2009). "Riflessioni sulle esperienze istituzionali di uno psicologo analista", *Rivista di Psicologia Analitica*, 79(27).

Malinconico, A. (2007). "Sognare, giocare, come risognare. Nuovi scenari per l'analisi junghiana", in *Il gesto che racconta. Setting analitico e Gioco della sabbia*, eds. A. Donfrancesco and M.A. Venier, Rome: Edizioni scientifiche.

Mastroianni, M. (2009). "L'intervallo ritrovato. Il setting nella cura analitica delle psicosi: misura, intenzione e opportunità", *Rivista di Psicologia Analitica*, 79(27).

Pattis Zoja, E., Castellana F. (2022) (eds.). *Sandplay e psicopatologie gravi*, Bergamo: Moretti e Vitali.

Pikes, N. (2005). *Dark Voices: The Genesis of Roy Hart Theatre* (2nd edn), New Orleans: Spring Journal Books.

Racamier, P.C. (1972). *Lo psicoanalista senza divano. La psicoanalisi e le strutture psichiatriche*, trans. from the original, *Le Psychanalyste sans divan*, Payot, Parigi, di Vera Varalda, Raffaello Cortina Editore, Milan (1982).

Recalcati, M. (2014). *La forza del desiderio*, Biella: Edizioni Qiqajon.

Ryce-Menuhin, J. (1992). *Jungian Sandplay. The Wonderful Therapy*, London and New York: Routledge; Italian edn., *Il gioco della sabbia. La terapia delle meraviglie*, ed. Annalisa Barbier, Rome: Edizioni Magi, 2004.

Tozzi, C. (2017). "Il viaggio del paziente sceneggiatore: dall'immaginazione attiva al linguaggio di un film", *Rivista di Psicologia Analitica*, 96(44).

Tozzi, C. (2017a). "A different way of being in the world: The attitude of the patient screenwriter", *Journal of Analytical Psychology*, 65(2).

Tozzi, C. (2020). "From horror to ethical responsibility: Carl Gustav Jung and Stephen King encounter the dark half within us, between us and in the world", *Journal of Analytical Psychology*, 65(1).

Vogler, C. (1992). *Il viaggio dell'Eroe. La struttura del mito ad uso di scrittori di narrativa e cinema*, trans. from the original, *The Writer's Journey: Mythic Structure for Writers* (Studio City, CA: Michael Wiese Productions) ed. Jusi Loreti, Rome: Dino Audino Editore, 1999; new edn. 2010.

Chapter 8

Yesterday, Today and Tomorrow

Active Imagination, Analytical
Training and Clinical Practice[1]

Marta Tibaldi

The supermarket of the psyche and over-the-counter psychology: this consumer image struck me, when, visiting the new office of a colleague, I spotted their patients – in the American style "clients" – in the waiting room, a group of men and women sitting all together, each queuing for their own particular therapist. Trained as I am to respect the setting and confidentiality, the busy scene made me immediately uncomfortable.[2] "Oh no," I thought. "Here we are in the supermarket of the psyche!" It was not an analytical office, and though the colleague in question was of a different professional background, I registered the difference between what could be called the "psychotherapeutic" and the "analytic psychological approach". In addition to a focus on the Ego, the latter involves a particularly responsible and careful relationship with the personal, archetypal and transpersonal unconscious aspects of the psyche. Here, within this broader, deeper perspective, the method of Active Imagination plays a fundamental role.

Many years go by and here we are in 2020, the *annus horribilis* of the Covid pandemic. Online psychotherapy explodes, and with it, many different offerings of therapies, support, counselling and so forth.

Psychologists discover the "market" of the psyche. On the web, everything is polished and sold through marketing techniques, raising professional visibility and attractiveness to clients, within the best neoliberal rules of "making anything a commodity". Consequently, social media advertises every kind of intervention. Psychology becomes increasingly fragmented. My discomfort deepens as the psychological market seems to sell more and more "hot water". For me, this psychological "giving to drink"[3] characterizing the collective pandemic and post-pandemic situation, admits us to the territory of Donizetti's *L'elisir d'amore*, Dulcamara hawking his fake love potion to Nemorino and directing its consumption be doubled.[4]The basic psycho-emotional and cultural skills that, up to a certain point, we considered as given in patients who sought to enter analysis (today we could simply call them "good manners" and "literacy"), are in fact, increasingly rare. Indeed, at the collective level, some of these basic, soft skills can be lacking to the degree they become psychopathological problems.[5] None of this is good.

DOI: 10.4324/9781003411369-8

Practising analysis is complex work, involving the personal, impersonal and transpersonal aspects of personality, both conscious and unconscious. As such, analysis deals with subjective suffering and psychopathology but, at the same time, considers the finalistic tendencies of the psyche and the creation of a personal cosmology.[6] For this reason, Jung differentiated "analytical psychology" from "complex psychology", distinguishing the psychopathological horizon from the search for the meaning of living and dying (not only human).[7] Doing Active Imagination presupposes the ability to recognize these differences, putting the Ego–Self axis in a reciprocal dialogue and confrontation: a challenging task, that has always been the goal of those interested in paths of wisdom, East and West.[8] Currently, this research is particularly difficult, having to face and overcome the collective tendency to reason with binary logic, unilateralism and hyper-simplification, linked to the general "illiteracy of return", and dramatically visible in the public sphere.[9] Therefore, when we speak of Active Imagination and desire to practise it, how far are we from the current, collective unawareness, whose horizon often tends to co-incide with the conscious prejudice, thereby losing the unconscious and complex aspects of the psyche?[10] The method of Active Imagination not only deals with all of this, it "risks" a radical confrontation with it.[11] Moreover, to practise it we need a personality "alchemically worked",[12] one that has built a reflective space between conscious and unconscious psyche and is aware of, and sensitive to, their existential dynamics. This is why for a long time in the analytical field, it was argued that Active Imagination could be done only at the end of personal analysis. Taking a different view, I propose imaginal dialogues even during analysis, albeit gradually, and in a manner tailored to the patient's ability to maintain good balance in the Ego–Self axis.

Beyond these general reflections, I would like to tell, now, my personal experience of Active Imagination. For a long time in Italy, or at least in Rome, where I trained,[13] it was looked at with the kind of circumspection that, perhaps, borders on suspicion. I remember how at AIPA (*Associazione Italiana di Psicologia Analitica*), when we talked about Active Imagination, we did so almost under our breath, at times even linking it to some of "Jung's psychotic aspects". The prevailing sense was here is something dangerous, expressing the more embarrassing aspects of analytical psychology, so better we let it go.[14] This echoed what had happened with the aspects of Ernst Bernhard's[15] way of doing analysis,[16] that at the time were considered "slippery". Italian analytical psychology, then, or at least as founded by AIPA,[17] favoured the psychiatric-clinical approach, to the detriment of the imaginary side, that in a certain collective vulgate, was linked to Jung's "mystic" aspects.[18] But how can we forget that Jung, himself, warned that when we do Active Imagination we put in place a "conscious psychosis"? An oxymoron? A contradiction in terms? Or rather the awareness that when we let the Self speak and confront the archetypal and transpersonal dynamics of psyche, we suspend, temporarily, the focus on the Ego complex, making it receptive to the totality of the psyche and letting it become, as von Franz writes, its "tool"?[19]

In 2010 the publication of *The Red Book* tore the veil on this way of knowing not just ourselves, but the world, the universe and our attitude to each. Since then, many things have changed. Suddenly, what in Jungian theory and practice had been viewed with a certain suspicion, became valued and welcomed. Here was a 180-degree rotation. As the "wrong stone" of Jung's tower in Bollingen[20] became the cornerstone of the building, Active Imagination emerged as that of our theoretical and clinical consideration.[21]

In this context, I would like to outline my personal, learning and teaching experience of Active Imagination. Professionally, this "story" has existed for than 40 years now. Personally, it has been integral to and from my early life.

From Personal Experiences to Professional Commitment

If we take Active Imagination to mean the comparison and direct dialogue between the Ego and unconscious images, then it is something I have experienced, albeit undefined, unlabelled, since childhood and my first memories of myself. Through a series of not-entirely fortunate events, resulting in overwhelming emotions, I urgently needed to find psychic resources for myself.[22] My way has been to personify and take an active position towards them: a natural training in Active Imagination, as a response to the unconscious experiences that "press from the subsoil", which Jung described in his *Memories*.[23] Therefore, I can say that both internal dialogues and imaginary presences have been a lifelong, rich resource and a fundamental part of my psychic development. Consequently, many years later when I discovered the method of Active Imagination *per se*, I found it immediately familiar and without the dangers that had been intimated. This, despite the fact that, professionally, in the years of my analytical training in Rome, Active Imagination tended to be something neither spoken of, nor experienced. Of course, we knew that in Zurich the method was taught and used, but I perceived a certain suspicion about the process and its practitioners. Moreover, Zurichers tended to be "imaginary"; that definition, itself, having an aura of negativity or prejudice.

That said, one of the founders of AIPA, Paolo Aite, had a marked sensitivity towards images, unusual among Roman analytical psychologists at that time. It was with him I had my first group analytical experience. This became my "Jungian baptism". The choice of analytical psychology and the motivation to commit to the profession would come later, having read an issue of the *Journal of Analytical Psychology*, entitled "Existing as a Woman".[24] Immediately I thought, "this is the work I want to do". And so I did it.[25]

In 1993 I took part in a group on Active Imagination, led by Federico De Luca Comandini,[26] with the warm, supportive presence of Bianca Garufi.[27] It was essential to explore the work with valued colleagues, who used the method and appreciated its importance. Federico De Luca Comandini had trained in Zurich where Active Imagination was recognized and treated with full theoretical and clinical dignity. Regarding Bianca Garufi, what to say? A vital figure on the Italian scene, she was for all of us who have known or attended her, a beacon of creativity and culture. Within AIPA she was an essential point of reference for professionals interested in psychic images and the active, creative and transformative relationship with them. Garufi had also lived in Hong Kong; the link with this city resurfacing in my life many years later.[28]

In that time, and in particular from 1993 onwards, I began publishing on the Active Imagination method, initially in the *Foglio Notizie AIPA* (News Sheet AIPA) and then on the IAAP Newsletter.[29] It was necessary to highlight, first, the dearth of familiarity with Active Imagination generally, and second, how marginalized it was in analytical training, both in theory and practice. To address this, we worked in the dual register – theoretical and experiential – sharing episodes of Active Imagination both personal and professional. We dealt, too, with issues such as the expansive or restrictive definition of the method and, critically, the difference between imaginative activity and Active Imagination, their being discrete phenomena. Our works also addressed the need to move awareness towards internal images and the transcendent function, discussing the optimum moment in analysis to propose Active Imagination as an experience, the role that the Ego complex can play with regard to archetypal images, together with possible risks and defence mechanisms. A further topic was the link or links between imagination and Sand-play, hoping for a comparison with colleagues who, at the time, were beginning to deal with this modality. Personally speaking, the use of handwriting to compare spontaneous images was gaining increasing importance in my relationship with the unconscious psyche, fully accepting what Jung states in *The Transcendent Function*: it is appropriate to transcribe by hand, on paper, our active imaginations, because writing gives an objective form to our internal world, making it visible from the outside.[30] Afterwards, my *Active Deep Writing*, a confrontation with the Ego complex and archetypal images, would formalize this approach. Something I will address later.

In 1995, I published in Italian "Jung in Comparison with the Unconscious: An Autobiographical Description of Active Imagination", my first paper on the method.[31] It was a reconstruction of the four phases of Active Imagination[32] in what Jung described as his "most difficult experiment" in the personal and professional crisis that led him to confront the unconscious directly, modifying his previous way of conceiving spontaneous images. They would no longer be assessed on the basis of their content, but by being attentive to the conscious attitude towards them, integrating this unconscious material into the individual vision of the world.[33]

One year later, in 1996, I had the opportunity to comment with Joan Chodorow on my way to "extract" from Jung's *Memories* these four phases and to reconstruct in this way the genesis and formalization of the method. In 1997, in her book *Jung on Active Imagination*, she would propose a similar autobiographical reading of it.[34] Over the years this paper of mine became my basic reference in illustrating and teaching the method of Active Imagination.

Having published further papers dealing, again, with the theme of writing and the confrontation with unconscious images,[35] in 1999 I held my first public presentation on Active Imagination. Entitled "Raping the Soul. An Example of Active Imagination",[36] it was presented at the 14th International Congress of Analytical Psychology in Florence.[37] Over the years, I wrote yet further articles, dealing with various aspects of the method, developing what would become my formalized way to confront the Ego–Self axis through handwriting (*Active Deep Writing*).[38] In 2011, after *The Red Book* was published in Italy, I proposed to the independent Roman publisher, Alessandro Orlandi, something that, at the time, was risky:[39] a book on the practice of Active Imagination, in which I would report actual, imaginary dialogues and address the theme of somatic, imaginal countertransference. Here, I am pleased to mention Angela Connolly, no longer with us, and who was, at the time, IAAP Vice-President. Presenting the book at AIPA, Angela Connolly emphasized, in particular, the importance of Active Imagination in relation to the somatic counter-transference. If little was said about the topic at the time, even less was written.[40] The 1995 article and the subsequent book were something new in Italian publishing, becoming a reference for trainees who subsequently learned and practised Active Imagination. In those years, too, there was a fruitful and significant exchange with Francesco Donfrancesco.[41] It was he who had brought James Hillman's thought and books to Italy. I took part in Donfrancesco's *Anima* seminars several times.[42]

Writing and Active Imagination

As I have said, in my personal research, and the learning and teaching of the method, handwriting has always been pivotal. Having published in 2004 "Double Objectivation and Formation of the Imaginal Ego" – my first attempt to systematize what became, later, one of the two ways to practise *Active Deep Writing* – in 2016 I published, in English and Italian, a paper with the same title. It was the opportunity to describe an analytical technique aimed at confronting the Ego-complex and unconscious images through handwriting. This modality distinguishes what pertains to the Ego complex ("Double objectivation") from what comes from the Self ("Archetypal writing"), stressing the eccentric point of "the observer", who must take responsibility and an ethical stand towards both the Ego and the Self: then differentiating all the "ingredients" necessary to make active imagination.[43]

These papers then, helped me to structure my way of teaching Active Imagination. Later, I would propose this theoretical and practical approach to the IAAP routers in Hong Kong and Taipei, Taiwan,[44] where I developed a six-hour teaching module. In time, this would be offered, also, to Italian trainees, the different cultural responses providing interesting comparison.[45]

The China of Hong Kong and Taiwan – at that time, two characteristic and discrete cultural realities – proved to be a highly favourable setting for teaching and practising Active Imagination. The local trainees were extremely interested, and thanks to their habitual practice of meditation, had no difficulty with the first two phases of the method, "emptying the mind" and "letting a spontaneous image emerge". The problem came when, having to focus on and "catch" that first spontaneous image, their meditative habit meant they tended to let it go. For the Italian students, the opposite was the case. With their different habit of hyper-investing in Ego, consciousness and the "thinking function", "making the void" could be difficult, even elusive.

My latest publication on the method is "Active Imagination, Extraversion, Cross-Culture. Guan Yin and Chinese Divination".[46] It addresses the way in which Chinese clients tend to practise divination, proposing to look at it as an extroverted form of Active Imagination. In my clinical practice with them, I noted their tendency to look at the Goddess Guan-Yin, address her as if she were present, which, from an analytical perspective, could be considered an active and direct dialogue with an archetypal image, itself an extroverted way to do Active Imagination. In parallel to these considerations, it is also worth remembering how, since the Eranos Conferences in Ancona, for Western Jungians, the way to confront Chinese divination – in particular the consultation of *The Book of Changes* (*I Ching*) – has become a central reference as a synchronistic experience. The interest of Western Jungians has produced a return effect on Chinese Jungians, who rediscovered *The Book of Changes* also in this respect.[47] Recently Matteo Sgorbati, in his book *L'I Ching a Eranos. Wilhelm, Jung e la ricezione del Classico dei Mutamenti*, describes how "the first of the Confucian classics" became part of the cultural references of Jungian tradition, being subsequently looked at with new eyes in China also, although with risks and contradictions, on both sides.[48]

Active Imagination and National and International Training

The institutional interest of AIPA towards the learning and teaching of Active Imagination, developing over time, accelerated in 2001 when the Ministry of Health recognized, legally, the psychotherapeutic school. Thereafter, courses were organized on the basis of the Ministerial directives. On AIPA's website you can read today (2022): "The school's training course is based on the principles of analytical psychology and deepens the study of the structure and the dynamics of the psyche, in its contents and its methods to explore it: dream, symbol, active imagination, sand-play."

In the first years after legal recognition of the school, I held several courses on dreams, images and Active Imagination, presenting various seminars on the method in Milan and Naples.[49] Through these, I defined and developed my teaching, incorporating, among other things, the genesis of the method, the presentation of the four phases, its diagnostic use, some practical exercises on how to begin, and the preparatory use of handwriting etc. With regard to the last two phases of the method, in particular – "setting a direct dialogue with the unconscious images" and "taking a responsible and ethical position towards them" – it was necessary to shift the teaching from a large audience to a small group or individuals. In principle, my lessons are tailored to a wider audience, while the direct practice of the method is necessarily limited to people already trained in small groups or in a personal context.

At the moment, five more meetings on the method are scheduled for analytical trainees and the general public in the AIPA's headquarters in Milan, as well for the China Society for Analytical Psychology (CSAP).[50] For both scenarios, my plan is to propose training modules. These would include preparatory use of *Active Deep Writing* in order to differentiate the "ingredients" of Active Imagination (Ego–Self–observer); theoretical and practical introduction to the method following its genesis, as told by Jung in his *Memories*; experiential workshops of the first two phases of the method and, for those who wish, the possibility to continue the imaginal practice in small groups and/or individually. Obviously, the international and transcultural context is a challenge, because the method must be calibrated according to local sensibilities and idiosyncrasies, giving attention to the "cultural unconscious" underlying the different contexts.[51]

A Side Note

I wrote this chapter in winter 2021–2022, during the fourth pandemic wave in Italy. The immense, traumatic experience of COVID-19 had widely affected people individually and collectively, pushing us Jungians to consider how best to conduct analysis at that moment and in the future. During the first year of the pandemic, my clinical approach focused, particularly, on the use of the alchemical metaphor as a grid to understand and process the traumatic experience in an imaginal form.[52] In the second year, the pandemic's move from acute trauma to chronic trauma demanded a shift in perspective from us practitioners. I returned to some of the non-analytical approaches I had used in the past, for example, bilateral stimulation,[53] together with the clinical application of the polyvagal theory, aimed at promoting a sense of deep security, at a time in which the collective and individual dysregulation was stressing the experience of danger. I am citing, particularly, my approach to integrating into the analytical setting, some elements derived from Francine Shapiro's *Adaptive Information Processing Model*[54] and Stephen W. Porges' *Polyvagal Theory*.[55] As we know, the active promotion of security, linked to feelings of well-being and bodily relaxation, can spur creativity and activate deep images. Just as Active Imagination teaches us not to have prejudices against any material emerging from the unconscious, I believe it can also open us up to other theories and practices, without an *a priori* or prejudicial stance. In fact, I am convinced that Jungian training could confront these new paradigms and tools with a distinct clinical advantage. If, 15 years ago, I began to reflect on the possibility of integrating into the analytical setting, bilateral stimulations (such as tapping) as activators of unconscious images, today I can affirm that some forms of psychoeducation and clinical application of the polyvagal theory, as a support to stabilize the Ego, are valuable in bringing relief to dysregulated states, not accessible verbally, preparing the ground for an imaginal and analytical work.[56] I believe, further, that the future of Active Imagination will be linked to our ability to confront and integrate knowledge and tools from evidence-based research and scientific knowledge unknown in the time of Jung. Current Jungian training could usefully integrate these theoretical references and clinical tools, to achieve the desired self-realization within the individuation process.

Conclusion

The story of my relationship with the method of Active Imagination is long and multi-faceted; from experiences as a child to professional sharing with colleagues; teaching in Italy to setting up transcultural modalities; using handwriting to create new synergies with other paradigms. The relationship is still evolving. Meanwhile, in my journey through Active Imagination, new interests have taken shape together with new directions of experimentation and research, to form a kind of clinical–theoretical hybrid. This propels me to a future in which Jungian deep analysis, specifically, with its ability to recognize and give voice to the personal, archetypal and transpersonal unconscious, can be enriched by the practical tools, the scientific and theoretical evidence of other paradigms. In much the same way as the globalized world presents us with challenges, asks us to find creative answers within epochal transformation, we could update analytical psychology by grafting new knowledge and skills derived from other perspectives on the psyche. More and more, the transcultural hybridization, understood in a broad sense, will reveal further an element of transformation. It will project us towards a future we do not yet know, but whose potential we are starting to glimpse: creative or destructive. The choice is ours.

Notes

1 This title takes up that of the homonymous film by Vittorio de Sica (*Ieri, oggi, domani*, 1963). This decision is to highlight the relationship I have had over time with the method of Active Imagination and my future trend lines about it.
2 As known, one of the first rules of the analytical setting is not to let patients meet with each other. See R. Laing, *The Technique of Psychoanalytic Psychotherapy*. New York: Jason Aronson, 1973–1974. Trans. R. Langs, *La tecnica della psicoterapia psicoanalitica*. Turin: Boringheri, 1979.
3 In Italian the expression "dare a bere" means to pass off as a real one.
4 "Udite, udite, o rustici/attenti, non fiatate/io già suppongo e immagino/ che al pari di me sappiate/ ch'io sono quel gran medico/dottore enciclopedico/ chiamato Dulcamara/ la cui virtù preclara/ e i portanti infiniti/ sono noti in tutto il mondo . . . e in altri siti/ [. . .] Comprate il mio specifico, /a poco ve lo do. [. . .] /(http://librettidopera.it).
5 I think, for example, of what after each summer is referred to as *summer blues* (or summer depression), that is the need to readapt to the rhythms of the city. It becomes obviously problematic (not pathologic!) if the holidays end close to the day when you resume work, without giving the body and mind the time to transit from one situation to another.
6 *Jung's Red Book. Creation of a New Cosmology* is the title of the exhibition organized in New York by the Rubin Museum of Art in 2009. On that occasion Jung's manuscript was exhibited for the first time to the public. See C.G. Jung, *The Red Book: Liber Novus*, New York and London: Norton & Co., 2009.
7 See R. Braidotti, *Il postumano. La vita oltre l'individuo, oltre la specie, oltre la morte*. Rome: DeriveApprodi, 2013. Trans. R. Braidotti, *The Posthuman*, Cambridge: Polity Press, 2013.

8　See C.G. Jung (1929/1957), "Commentary to The Secret of The Golden Flower", *Psyche and Religion: West and East*, CW11. Princeton NJ: Princeton University Press, 1970. Trans. C.G. Jung (1929/1957), "Commento al Segreto del Fiore d'Oro", *Studi sull'alchimia*, OC13. Turin: Boringhieri, 1988.

9　By *return illiteracy* we mean "that share of literate people who, without the exercise of alphanumeric skills, regresses, losing the ability to use written language to formulate messages" (www.treccani.it).

10　Never as in the pandemic have we witnessed the so-called Dunning-Kruger effect, or the ignorance of not knowing, overestimating in a completely arbitrary way one's skills and competence. See M. Tibaldi, "Sapere di non sapere. L'effetto Dunning-Kruger" – http://martatibaldi.blogspot.com – 4 November 2019.

11　Think of the radicality of Jung's experience in *The Red Book. Liber Novus*.

12　I refer to the "transmutations" described by the alchemical metaphor, that is, to the different psychic transformations, that are linked to the confrontation with the unconscious material. See. S. Massa Ope, A. Rossi, M. Tibaldi, *Jung e la metafora viva dell'alchimia. Immagini della trasformazione psichica*. Bergamo: Moretti & Vitali, 2020. See also M. Tibaldi and S. Massa Ope, *Pandemia e trasformazione. Un anno per rinascere*. Bergamo: Moretti & Vitali, 2021.

13　I refer to the analytical training of *Associazione Italiana di Psicologia Analitica* (AIPA) in Rome in the 1980s and 1990s.

14　This difficulty perhaps also came from the fact that the founders of AIPA didn't have personal experience of Active Imagination.

15　Ernst Bernhard was a Jewish doctor. He lived in Rome from 1945 to 1965 and was the first President of *Associazione Italiana di Psicologia Analitica* (AIPA). Among his patients were Federico Fellini, Natalia Ginzburg, Adriano Olivetti, Giorgio Manganelli, Cristina Campo, Allan Tate.

16　I refer to some aspects of his way of doing analysis that were considered "esoteric": astrology, palmistry, Chinese divination.

17　On the AIPA website you can read: "The Association, the first Italian company member of IAAP, was founded on May 26, 1961 [. . .] The headquarters were in Rome, the President Ernst Bernhard; Gianfranco Tedeschi, Treasurer. He became the second President at the death of Bernhard in 1966. [. . .] Among the first analysts of the analytical training organized by AIPA we remember: Paolo Aite, Giuseppe Donadio, Hélène Erba-Tissot, Bianca Garufi, Antonino Lo Cascio, Marcello Pignatelli, Michele Pignatelli di Cerchiara, Anna Quagliata."

18　See G. Lachman, *Jung the Mystic: The Esoteric Dimension of Carl Gustav Jung's Life and Teaching*. New York: TarcherPerigee, 2012. Trans. G. Lachman, *Jung il mistico. Dimensioni esoteriche della vita e degli insegnamenti di Carl G. Jung*. Rome: Mediterranee, 2012.

19　See M.-L. von Franz, *Alchemy: An Introduction to the Symbolism and the Psychology*. Toronto, Canada: Inner City Books, 1982. Trans. M.-L. von Franz, *Alchimia*. Torino: Bollati Boringhieri, 1984.

20　The Bollingen Tower is a stone construction that Jung built in the countryside of San Meinrad at the top of Lake Zurich. The Tower was his elective place where he spent about half the year (See C.G. Jung, *Jung's Memories, Dreams, Reflections* (ed. By A. Jaffé). London: Fontana Press, 1995. Trans. C.G. Jung, *Ricordi, sogni, riflessioni di C.G. Jung* (a c. di A. Jaffé). Milan: BUR, 1978.

21　Jung writes: "I lived as if under constant inner pressure. At times this became so strong that I suspected there was some psychic disturbance in myself" (p. 197), "An incessant stream of fantasies had been released, and I did my best not to lose my head but to find some way to understand these strange things. I stood helpless before an alien world; everything in it seemed difficult and incomprehensible. I was living in a constant state of tension; often I felt as if gigantic blocks of stone were tumbling down upon me. My enduring these storms was a question of brute strength" (ivi, p. 201).

22 My personal traumatic experiences have made me question several critical issues of a certain way of doing analysis. See M. Tibaldi, "A proposito del 'fare analisi'", *Postfazione* a E. Ambrosi, *Inconscio ladro. Le malefatte degli psicoanalisti*. Rome: La Lepre, 2010. See also M. Tibaldi, "Trauma zero. Storia di un lutto complesso non guarito". In A. Onofri, C. La Rosa (a c. di), *Dal basso in alto (e ritorno). Nuovi approcci bottom-up: psicoterapia cognitiva, corpo, EMDR*. Rome: Apertamenteweb, 2018, pp. 311–318.

23 See C.G. Jung, *Jung's Memories, Dreams, Reflection*.

24 *Rivista di Psicologia Analitica*, "Esistere, come donna", n. 16/1977. Venezia: Marsilio, 1977.

25 Of this experience and of how its transformative trace has been reactivated in the time of pandemic, see M. Tibaldi, "Esistere come donna", in M. Tibaldi, S. Massa Ope, *Pandemia e trasformazione. Un anno per rinascere*, pp. 91–101.

26 Federico De Luca Comandini is a Jungian analyst. He graduated in the C.G. Jung Institut in Zurich and was trained by Dieter Baumann and Marie-Louise von Franz.

27 Bianca Garufi, a writer, poet and Jungian analyst has been a leading figure in the Italian cultural scene. She was loved by Cesare Pavese, who dedicated her *Dialoghi con Leucò* (Turin: Einaudi, 2014). Together they wrote *Fuoco Grande* (Turin: Einaudi, 2008).

28 Hong Kong is a city that I loved very much, in which I had the opportunity to stay several times in the years in which I held the position of Liaison Person IAAP. See M. Tibaldi, "Hong Kong, the beloved" – http://martatibaldi.blogspot.com – 11 October 2019.

29 M. Tibaldi, "Immaginazione attiva come spazio di libertà", *Foglio Notizie AIPA*, n. 15/1993, pp. 43–45; M. Tibaldi "Il gruppo sull'immaginazione attiva", *Foglio Notizie AIPA*, n. 16/1994, pp. 32–33; M. Tibaldi, "Some News Regarding a Study Group in Rome on Active Imagination", *Newsletter IAAP*, n. 15/1995.

30 See C.G. Jung (1916–1958), *The Transcendent Function*, CW8. Princeton NJ: Princeton University Press, 1970.

31 M. Tibaldi, "Jung a confronto con l'inconscio: una descrizione autobiografica del metodo dell'immaginazione attiva". *Studi Junghiani*, n 2/1995, pp. 141–159.

32 When I talk about "four phases", I refer to Marie Louise von Franz's systematization of the method. In an essay of hers, considered a classic on Active Imagination, she describes the four phases as follows: 1st phase "emptying one's mind of the thought processes of the Ego"; 2nd phase "bringing a fantastic unconscious image into the field of internal attention"; 3rd phase "providing some form of expression to fantasy"; 4th phase "it consists in the ethical comparison with whatever one has previously produced" (see M.L. von Franz, "L'immaginazione attiva". *Rivista di Psicologia Analitica*, 17/1978, pp. 75–87).

33 See C.G. Jung (1952), *Symbols of Transformation*, CW5. London: Routledge, 1956. Trans. *Simboli della trasformazione*, OC5. Turin: Boringhieri, 1970.

34 See J. Chodorow, *Jung on Active Imagination*. Princeton NJ: Princeton University Press, 1977.

35 See M. Tibaldi, "Psicologia analitica, esperienza della scrittura e conoscenza di sé". *Rivista di Psicologia analitica*, n. 52/1995, pp. 19–31; M. Tibaldi, "Il confronto etico con le immagini inconsce, lo sviluppo della funzione sentimento e la creazione di sistemi di valore". *Studi Junghiani*, n. 5/1977, pp. 140–143.

36 M. Tibaldi, "Raping the Soul. An Experience of Active Imagination". *Proceedings of the Fourteenth International Congress for Analytical Psychology* (edited by M.A. Matoon). Einsiedeln, Switzerland: Daimon Verlag, 1999, pp. 208–219.

37 It was the XIV International Congress of Analytical psychology "Destruction and Creation: Personal and Cultural Transformation", which took place in Florence in 1998.

38 See M. Tibaldi, "In forma narrativa. Scrittura autobiografica dell'anima", in AA.VV. *Un oscuro impulso interiore (Anima)*. Bergamo: Moretti & Vitali, 1999, pp. 71–81;

M. Tibaldi, "La passione narrativa. Appunti per una scrittura autobiografica dell'anima", in AA.VV. *Per nascosti sentieri (Anima)*. Bergamo: Moretti & Vitali, 2001, pp. 191–206; M. Tibaldi, "Sintomi e immagini", in AA.VV., *Genitori e figli. Conoscere per avvicinarsi*. Roma: Edizioni Universitarie Romane 2001, pp. 101–106; M. Tibaldi, "Come iniziare il confronto con le immagini inconsce. Due esempi di immaginazione attiva", in AA.VV. *Immaginazione attiva* (a c. di F. De Luca Comandini e B. Mercurio), Milano: Vivarium 2002, pp. 119–126; M. Tibaldi, "Immagini cinematografiche e costruzione dell'Io immaginale. Lo psicologo analista tra immagini esterne e immagini interne", in AA.VV. *Ciak. Si vive. Grande schermo e piccoli gruppi*. Roma: Magi Edizioni, 2004, pp. 67–71; M. Tibaldi, "Doppia oggettivazione e formazione dell'Io immaginale", in AA.VV., *Alchimie della formazione analitica* (a c. di G.M. Cerbo, D. Palliccia, A.M. Sassone). Milano: Vivarium, 2004, pp. 329–338; M. Tibaldi, "L'intero universo è un'unica perla brillante. Un approccio junghiano alla scrittura autobiografica del profondo nell'esperienza oncologica", in D. Demetrio, C. Borgonovi (a c. di), *Adultità, scrittura e terapia*, n. 27. Milano: Guerini, 2007, pp. 53–69; M. Tibaldi, "Nuvole nel cielo, comunque si indovina la luna", in F. Donfrancesco (ed.) (Anima), *Perdita e ricerca del centro*. Bergamo: Moretti & Vitali, 2009, pp. 119–142.

39 See M. Tibaldi, *Marta Tibaldi – Psicologia analitica in un click – YouTube – Pratica dell'immaginazione attiva. Dialogare con l'inconscio e vivere meglio*: https://www.youtube.com/watch?v=g7l_1tAZCOA&t=3s

40 The theme was taken up several years later by Salvatore Martini in the paper: S. Martini, "Embodying analysis: the body and the therapeutic process". *Journal of Analytical Psychology*, 61(1), pp. 5–23, with which in 1997 he won the Fordham Award.

41 Francesco Donfrancesco, medical doctor and Jungian analyst, in 1988 founded the Journal *Anima*, that he directed until 2012. He edited papers and books by James Hillman and by other authors of archetypal psychology. His writings have been translated in Brazil, England and United States. In 2000 he won the *Gradiva Award for Essays and Articles*.

42 In addition to the articles already listed in footnote 37, see also M. Tibaldi, "La pratica delle immagini", in *James Hillman. Verso il sapere dell'anima* (ed. F. Donfrancesco). *Anima*, October 2012, pp. 347–360; M. Tibaldi, "Practicing Images. Clinical Implications of James Hillman's Theory in a Multicultural Reality and in a Changing World", in *Analytical Psychology in a Changing World: The Search for Self, Identity and Community* (edited by L. Huskinson and M. Stein). London: Routledge, 2014, pp. 147–160; M. Tibaldi, "Practising Analytical Psychology in East Asia: A Post-Jungian Italian Perspective". *Psychoanalysis and Psychotherapy in China*, vol. 1, 2015, pp. 78–96.

43 See M. Tibaldi, "Active Deep Writing – Scrittura attiva profonda", in *L'Ombra. Epistemologia dopo il Libro Rosso*, Bergamo: Moretti & Vitali, 2017, pp. 179–192; M. Tibaldi "Active Deep Writing". *Proceedings of the XX International Congress of Analytical Psychology* "Anima Mundi in Transition: Cultural, Clinical and Professional Challenges". Einsiedeln, Switzerland: Daimon Verlag, 2017, pp. 1269–1277.

44 In 2021 in recognition of the work done in favour of the future IAAP Taiwanese Society, I was appointed as an Honorary Member of the Taiwanese Society of Analytical Psychology (TSAP).

45 See M. Tibaldi et al., *Transcultural Identities. Jungians in Hong Kong*. Rome: Artemide, 2016.

46 See M. Tibaldi, "Active Imagination, Extraversion, Cross-Culture. Guan Yin and Chinese Divination", *Psychoanalysis and Psychotherapy in China*, 3(2), Winter 2020, pp. 278–288.

47 See "Jung across Cultural Borders", *The 2013 International Jungian Conference in Taiwan, October 17–20, 2013 –Encountering Taoism through The Red Book. The Asian Perspectives on Richard Wilhelm. East–West Dialogues. Jung, Asia and Interculture*.

48 See M. Sgorbati, *L'I Ching a Eranos. Wilhelm, Jung e la ricezione del* Classico dei mutamenti. Naples: oxp, 2021.

49 There are the annual courses "Sogni e tecnica interpretativa" (2008–2011), "Immagini e relazione analitica" (2010–2011), "Metodi e tecniche analitiche: l'immaginazione attiva" and "Il metodo dell'immaginazione attiva", "Il metodo dell'immaginazione attiva di C.G. Jung. Teoria, pratica e implicazioni cliniche" (2010–2015) carried out for students in the fourth and fifth year of AIPA's training school. "Tre seminari sull'immaginazione attiva in teoria e in pratica" (AIPA, Napoli October–December 2014); "Tre seminari sull'immaginazione attiva in teoria e in pratica" (AIPA, Milan, April-June 2015); "Immaginazione attiva: la pratica del metodo attraverso la lettura di alcuni scritti scelti di C.G. Jung" (AIPA, Milan, September–December 2015).

50 Four seminars on active imagination ("Active Imagination. A Daydream Process") are scheduled between February and October 2022.

51 See M. Tibaldi et al., *Transcultural Identities. Jungians in Hong Kong*. See also T. Singer, *Focus on Jung, Politics and Culture* (3 vols.). London: Routledge, 2020.

52 See M. Tibaldi, S. Massa Ope, *Pandemia e trasformazione. Un anno per rinascere*.

53 See M. Tibaldi, "Psicologia analitica ed EMDR: un avvicinamento possibile?". *Studi Junghiani*, 20(2), 2004, pp. 127–144. See also M. Tibaldi, *Jungian Analysis and EMDR: A Possible Rapprochement?* – http://martatibaldi.blogspot.com – 29 August 2018; M. Tibaldi, "Un processo creativo di nuove sintesi. EMDR e analisi junghiana", in M. Balbo (ed.), *EMDR: uno strumento di dialogo fra le psicoterapie*. Milan: McGraw-Hill, 2006, pp. 85–116.

54 See F. Shapiro, *Eye Movement Desensitization and Reprocessing (EMDR) Therapy: Basic Principles, Protocols and Procedures*. New York: Guilford Press, 2018. Trans. F. Shapiro, *EMDR. Il manuale. Principi fondamentali, protocolli e procedure*. Milan: Cortina, 2019.

55 See S.W. Porges, *The Polyvagal Theory*. New York and London: Norton & Company, 2011. Trans. S.W. Porges, *La teoria polivagale. Fondamenti neurofisiologici delle emozioni, dell'attaccamento, della comunicazione e dell'autoregolazione*. Rome: Fioriti, 2014. See also S.W. Porges and D. Dana, *Clinical Application of the Polyvagal Theory: The Emergence of Polyvagal Informed Therapies*. New York: Norton & Co, 2018. Trans. *Le applicazioni cliniche della teoria polivagale*. Roma: Fioriti, 2020.

56 See A. Damasio, *Feeling & Knowing. Making Minds Conscious*. New York: Pantheon, 2021. Trans. A. Damasio, *Sentire e conoscere. Storia delle menti coscienti*. Milan: Adelphi, 2022.

References

Analfabetismo in www.treccani.it

Braidotti, R., *Il postumano. La vita oltre l'individuo, oltre la specie, oltre la morte*. Rome: DeriveApprodi, 2013. Trans. R. Braidotti, *The Posthuman*. Cambridge: Polity Press, 2013.

Chodorow, J., *Jung on Active Imagination*. Princeton NJ: Princeton University Press, 1977.

Damasio, A., *Feeling & Knowing. Making Minds Conscious*. New York: Pantheon 2021. Trans. Damasio, A., *Sentire e conoscere. Storia delle menti coscienti*. Milan: Adelphi, 2022.

Donizetti, G., *L'elisir d'amore*, http://librettidopera.it

Garufi, B., Pavese, C., *Fuoco grande*. Turin: Einaudi, 2008.

Jung, C.G., "The Transcendent Function", *Structure and Dynamics of the Psyche*, CW 8. Princeton NJ: Princeton University Press, 2014. Trans. C.G. Jung (1916–1958), "La funzione trascendente", *La dinamica dell'inconscio*, OC8. Turin: Boringhieri, 1976.

Jung, C.G., "Commentary to The Secret of the Golden Flower", *Psyche and Religion: West and East*, CW11. Princeton NJ: Princeton University Press, 1970. Trans. C.G. Jung

(1929/1957), "Commento a Il Segreto del Fiore d'oro", *Studi sull'alchimia*, OC13. Turin: Boringhieri, 1988.

Jung, C.G., *Symbols of Transformation*, CW5. Princeton NJ: Princeton University Press, 1967. Trans. C.G. Jung (1952), *Simboli della trasformazione*, OC5. Turin: Boringhieri, 1970.

Jung, C.G., *Jung's Memories, Dreams, Reflections* (ed. A. Jaffé). London: Fontana Press, 1995. Trans. *Ricordi, sogni, riflessioni di C.G. Jung*, ed. A. Jaffé. Milan: BUR, 1978.

Jung, C.G., *The Red Book: Liber Novus*. New York and London: Norton & Co, 2009. Trans. C.G. Jung, *Il Libro Rosso. Liber Novus*. Turin: Bollati Boringhieri, 2010.

Lachman, G., *Jung the Mystic: The Esoteric Dimension of Carl Gustav Jung's Life and Teaching*. New York: Tarcher Perigee, 2012. Trans. G. Lachman, *Jung il mistico. Dimensioni esoteriche della vita e degli insegnamenti di Carl Gustav Jung*. Rome: Mediterranee, 2021.

Langs, R., *The Technique of Psychoanalytic Psychotherapy*. New York: Jason Aronson, 1973–1974. Trans. R. Langs, *La tecnica della psicoterapia psicoanalitica*. Turin: Boringhieri, 1979.

Martini, S., "Embodying Analysis: The Body and the Therapeutic Process". *Journal of Analytical Psychology*, 61(1), pp. 5–23.

Massa Ope, S., Rossi, A. Tibaldi, M. (eds.), *Jung e la metafora viva dell'alchimia. Immagini della trasformazione psichica*. Bergamo: Moretti & Vitali, 2021.

Pavese, C., *Dialoghi con Leucò*. Turin: Einaudi, 2014.

Porges, S.W., *The Polyvagal Theory*. New York and London: Norton & Co., 2011. Trans. S.W. Porges, *La teoria polivagale. Fondamenti neurofisiologici delle emozioni, dell'attaccamento, della comunicazione e dell'autoregolazione*. Rome: Fioriti, 2014.

Porges, S.W., Dana, D., *Clinical Applications of the Polyvagal Theory: The Emergence of Polyvagal Informed Therapies*. New York and London: Norton & Co., 2018. Trans. S.W. Porges and D. Dana, *Le applicazioni cliniche della teoria polivagale*, Rome: Fioriti, 2020.

Rivista di Psicologia Analitica: "Esistere come donna", 16, 1977. Venice: Marsilio, 1977.

Sgorbati, M., *L'I* Ching *a Eranos. Wilhelm, Jung e la ricezione del* Classico dei mutamenti. Naples: oxp, 2021.

Shamdasani, S., *The Red Book. Liber Novus*, in C.G. Jung, *The Red Book. Liber Novus*. New York and London: Norton & Co., 2009. Trans. S. Shamdasani, "Liber Novus – Il 'Libro Rosso' di C.G. Jung", in C.G. Jung, *Il Libro Rosso – Liber Novus*. Torino: Bollati Boringhieri, 2010.

Shapiro, F., *Eye Movement Desensitization and Reprocessing (EMDR) Therapy: Basic Principles, Protocols and Procedures*. New York: Guilford Press, 2018. Trans. F. Shapiro, *EMDR. Il manuale. Principi fondamentali, protocolli e procedure*. Milan: Cortina, 2019.

Singer, T., *Focus on Jung, Politics and Culture* (3 vols.). London: Routledge, 2020.

Tibaldi, M. "Il gruppo sull'immaginazione attiva". *Foglio Notizie AIPA*, 16, 1994, pp. 32–33.

Tibaldi, M. "Immaginazione attiva come spazio di libertà". *Foglio Notizie AIPA*, 15, 1993, pp. 43–45.

Tibaldi, M. "Jung a confronto con l'inconscio. Una descrizione autobiografica del metodo dell'immaginazione attiva". *Studi Junghiani*, 2, 1995, pp. 141–159.

Tibaldi, M. "Psicologia analitica, esperienza della scrittura e conoscenza di sé", *Rivista di Psicologia analitica*, 52, 1995, pp. 19–31.

Tibaldi, M. "Some News Regarding a Study Group in Rome on Active Imagination". *Newsletter IAAP*, 15, 1995.

Tibaldi, M., "A proposito del 'fare analisi'", "Postfazione" a E. Ambrosi, *Inconscio ladro. Le malefatte degli psicoanalisti.* Rome: La Lepre, 2010.

Tibaldi, M., "Practising Images. Clinical implications of James Hillman's Theory in a Multicultural Reality and in a Changing World". *Analytical Psychology in a Changing World: The Search for Self, Identity and Community* (eds. L. Huskinson and M. Stein). London: Routledge, 2014, pp. 147–160.

Tibaldi, M. "Practising Analytical Psychology in East Asia: A Post-Jungian Italian Perspective". *Psychoanalysis and Psychotherapy in China*, vol. 1, 2015, pp. 78–96.

Tibaldi, M., *"Active Deep Writing* – Scrittura attiva profonda". *L'Ombra. Epistemologia dopo il Libro Rosso.* Bergamo: Moretti & Vitali, 2017, pp. 179–192.

Tibaldi, M., "Active Deep Writing". *Proceedings of the XX International Congress of Analytical Psychology* "Anima Mundi in Transition: Cultural, Clinical and Professional Challenges". Einsiedeln, Switzerland: Daimon Verlag, 2017, pp. 1269–1277.

Tibaldi, M., "Active Imagination, Extraversion, Cross-Culture. Guan-Yin and Chinese Divination". *Psychoanalysis and Psychotherapy in China*, 3(2), Winter 2020, pp. 278–288.

Tibaldi, M., "Come iniziare il confronto con le immagini inconsce. Due esempi di immaginazione attiva", in AA.VV., *Immaginazione attiva* (eds. F. De Luca Comandini e R. Mercurio). Milan: Vivarium, 2002, pp. 119–126.

Tibaldi, M., "Doppia oggettivazione e formazione dell'Io immaginale", in AA.VV., *Alchimie della formazione analitica* (eds. G.M. Cerbo, D. Palliccia, A.M. Sassone). Milan: Vivarium, 2004, pp. 329–338.

Tibaldi, M., "Hong Kong, the Beloved", http://martatibaldi.blogspot.com – 11 October 2019.

Tibaldi, M., "Il confronto etico con le immagini inconsce, lo sviluppo della funzione sentimento e la creazione di sistemi di valore". *Studi Junghiani*, 5, 1997, pp. 140–143.

Tibaldi, M., "Immaginazione attiva come spazio di libertà". *Foglio Notizie AIPA*, 15, 1993, pp. 43–45.

Tibaldi, M., "Immagini cinematografiche e costruzione dell'Io immaginale. Lo psicologo analista tra immagini esterne e immagini interne", in *Ciak. Si vive. Grande schermo e piccoli gruppi.* Rome: Magi edizioni, 2004, pp. 67–71.

Tibaldi, M., "In forma narrativa. Scrittura autobiografica dell'anima", in AA.VV. *Un oscuro impulso interiore (Anima).* Bergamo: Moretti & Vitali, 1999, pp. 71–81.

Tibaldi, M., "Jung a confronto con l'inconscio: una descrizione autografica del metodo dell'immaginazione attiva". *Studi Junghiani*, 2, 1995, pp. 141–159.

Tibaldi, M., "L'intero universo è un'unica perla brillante. Un approccio junghiano alla scrittura autobiografica del profondo nell'esperienza oncologica", in D. Demetrio, C. Borgonovi (eds.), *Adultità, scrittura e terapia*, n. 27. Milan: Guerini, 2007, pp. 53–69.

Tibaldi, M., "La passione narrativa. Appunti per una scrittura autobiografica dell'anima", in AA.VV. *Per nascosti sentieri (Anima).* Bergamo: Moretti & Vitali, 2001, pp. 191–206.

Tibaldi, M., "La pratica delle immagini", in *James Hillman. Verso il sapere dell'anima* (ed. F. Donfrancesco). *Anima*, October 2012, pp. 347–360.

Tibaldi, M., "Nuvole nel cielo, comunque si indovina la luna", in F. Donfrancesco (ed.), *Anima, perdita e ricerca del centro.* Bergamo: Moretti & Vitali, 2009, pp. 119–142.

Tibaldi, M., "Psicologia analitica ed EMDR: un avvicinamento possibile?". *Studi Junghiani*, 20(2), 2004, pp. 127–144.

Tibaldi, M., "Psicologia analitica, esperienza della scrittura e conoscenza di sé". *Rivista di Psicologia analitica*, 52, 1995, pp. 19–31.

Tibaldi, M., "Raping the Soul. An Experience of Active Imagination", in *Proceedings of the Fourteenth International Congress for Analytical Psychology,* "Destruction and Creation: Personal and Cultural Transformation" (ed. M.A. Matoon). Eisedeln, Switzerland: Daimon Verlag, 1999, pp. 208–219.

Tibaldi, M., "Sapere di non sapere. L'effetto Dunning-Kruger" – http://martatibaldi.blogspot.com – 4 November 2019.

Tibaldi, M., "Sintomi e immagini", in AA.VV., *Genitori e figli. Conoscere per avvicinarsi.* Rome: Edizioni Universitarie Romane, 2001, pp. 101–106.

Tibaldi, M., "*Some News regarding a Study Group in Rome on Active Imagination*", *Newsletter IAAP,* n. 15/1995.

Tibaldi, M., "Trauma zero. Storia di un lutto complesso non guarito", in A. Onofri, C. La Rosa (eds.), *Dal basso in alto (e ritorno . . .). Nuovi approcci* bottom-up*: psicoterapia cognitiva, corpo, EMDR.* Rome: Apertamenteweb, 2017, pp. 311–318.

Tibaldi, M., "Un processo creativo di nuove sintesi. EMDR e analisi junghiana", in M. Balbo (ed.), *EMDR: uno strumento di dialogo fra le psicoterapie.* Milan: McGraw-Hill, 2006, pp. 85–116.

Tibaldi, M., Jungian analysis and EMDR: A Possible Rapprochement? – http://martatibaldi.blogspot.com – 29 August 2018.

Tibaldi, M., *Marta Tibaldi. Psicologia analitica in un click* – YouTube – *Pratica dell'immaginazione attiva. Dialogare con l'inconscio e vivere meglio.* https://www.youtube.com/watch?v=g7l_1tAZCOA&t=3s

Tibaldi, M., Massa Ope, S., *Pandemia e trasformazione. Un anno per rinascere.* Bergamo: Moretti & Vitali, 2021.

Tibaldi, M., *Pratica dell'immaginazione attiva. Dialogare con l'inconscio e vivere meglio.* Rome: La Lepre, 2010.

Tibaldi, M. et al., *Transcultural Identities. Jungians in Hong Kong.* Rome: Artemide Edizioni, 2016.

von Franz, M.-L., *Alchemy: An Introduction to the Symbolism and the Psychology.* Toronto: Inner City Books, 1982. Trans. M.-L. von Franz, *Alchimia,* Turin: Bollati Boringhieri, 1984.

Chapter 9

Symbols of the Soul

From *The Red Book* to Active Imagination in Movement

Antonella Adorisio

Active Imagination and *The Red Book*

Jung developed the method of active imagination over the course of a slow process that lasted his entire lifetime. Although Jung didn't collect all of his reflections in a single volume on the topic of active imagination, his reflections recurred consistently in many of his writings in a span of about 40 years. The first references are found in the essay "The Transcendent Function", written in 1916 and published in 1958; the last references are found in *Mysterium Coniunctionis* published in 1956. From the point of view of theoretic formulation, it took him about 20 years to arrive at an organic statement about the method that, in the course of the successive 20 years, was subject to additional examination and elaboration. Across his own experience and that of his patients, Jung created a form of meditation based essentially on the internal dialogue with the personifications of the unconscious. Active imagination is in fact a dialogue between the ego and the unconscious, a powerful and efficient method to turn the gaze towards the invisible world of our inner being. It's a central psychological and self-reflective inclination that promotes the use of the symbolic function in the internal encounter with the Other. Given the space and form to the implicit tension in the contrast of divergent positions, active imagination proposes the creation of unified symbols, that in the containment and transcendence of both opposites, can indicate new possibilities and facilitate the process of individuation.

The development of the method is strictly connected to the work Jung did on himself, in particular his intense experiences with the unconscious that characterize the years 1912–1917, a time when he underwent a deep inner crisis about which we have direct testimony thanks to the publication of *The Red Book*. In his *Memories*, Jung had already amply narrated the great importance of this path and had informed us that it took him well over 20 years before he began to truly comprehend the contents of those imaginations. Being able to read *The Red Book* makes one easily realize the extent to which the development of his thought drew vital nourishment from his intense confrontation with the unconscious.

It was important for Jung to let the contents of the unconscious emerge without hastily needing to seek a logical explanation. In the conclusion of "The

DOI: 10.4324/9781003411369-9

Transcendent Function", he reminds us that it's useful to wonder how a determined figure of the unconscious affects us. If the answer is immediate and natural, it will certainly be valid. If it isn't, then it's not important that the confrontation becomes immediately and totally conscious. Jung says: "In such cases one must be content with the wordless but suggestive feelings which appear in their stead and are more valuable than clever talk."[1] In *The Red Book*, he tells us what the Spirit of the Depth told him: "To understand a thing is a bridge and possibility of returning to the path. But to explain a matter is arbitrary and sometimes even murder. Have you counted the murderers among the scholars?"[2]

I wanted to emphasize how these quotes give us an idea of the attitude to adopt when we are put in relationship with our own internal images. A first important consideration is that the tendency to find a rational explanation kills the symbolic experience, and for this reason, in order to avoid stopping an ongoing process, active imaginations cannot be interpreted. They are lived through all the way, until the effects can be seen. Reading *The Red Book*, one continually comes across Jung's tireless search for sense, which makes one confront the necessity to welcome the nonsense as an unescapable part of the Supreme Meaning. "Nothing will deliver you from disorder and meaninglessness, since this is the other half of the world."[3]

In *The Red Book*, Jung experiences an inner conflict as he fights against his own contempt for his imaginary activities. As he battles the overconfidence of his intellect, he begins to trust the images and his unconscious. Thus he understands that the intellect, as part of the Whole, cannot explain everything because life is both rational and irrational. In this book, as he suffers from his internal conflict, he underscores the value of loss and of the non-power. In doing so, the heroic point of view is re-balanced against the triumph of the spirit of time which has unleashed wars of total projection of the Shadow and generated the conviction that the enemy was only outside. Jung tells us that by enduring and living through an inner civil war, one can recognize the enemy outside as a brother. During his visions, at times horrific, Jung realizes he assassinated and sacrificed the heroic principle, incarnate in the spirit of the time. From this moment, he crosses a path which causes him to endure a tumultuous internal conflict, an intimate war within himself. Due to this path, Jung understands that the hero represents absolutism and ideal perfection. Upon the death of the hero, it is possible to awaken to the fullness of life, becoming aware of the relativity of values, concepts and theories. In Jung's experience a new God can only be born once the hero is killed unintentionally and without willpower. Jung notes that the archetypal forms change according to the historical moment. In *The Red Book*, after having told us that Gods get older and the great truths become lies, he proceeds: "our Gods want to be overcome, since they require renewal".[4]

With its contempt of the irrational, the heroic spirit of time turned off the knowledge of the heart. Due to this, the spirit of the depth intervenes to limit with non-power the heroic spirit. The non-power helps us change our point of view, widen our perspective and facilitate transformation. Jung opens himself to the integrated knowledge of the heart through his words: the knowledge of the heart "is in no book and is not to be found in the mouth of any teacher, but grows out of you, like the green seed from the dark earth". [5]

In *The Red Book*, with the death of the heroic model, the necessity for imitation and the simian part of man fails. Everyone is unique and must be able to follow their own path.

> What is to come will be created in you and from you. Hence look into yourself. Do not compare, do not measure. No other way is like yours. All other ways deceive and tempt you. You must fulfill the way that is in you.[6]

The method of active imagination therefore discourages giving power to erudite and intellectual knowledge, to judgement or to the derision of our rationality, and invites us to welcome the fact that the most absurd can emerge, in tolerance of nonsense and non-power. Due to the dialogues with the personifications of the unconscious, Jung realized that he had attempted to imprison the soul in conceptual categories.

In 1913, the year of his separation from Freud, his soul was imposed as psychic reality and permitted Jung to reach a psychology that is explained by the soul. Jung's words couldn't be more clear:

> I still labored misguidedly under the spirit of this time, and thought differently about the human soul. I thought and spoke a lot about the soul. I knew many learned words for her, I had judged her and turned her into a scientific object. I did not consider that my soul cannot be the object of my judgment and knowledge; much more are my judgment and knowledge the objects of my soul. Therefore the spirit of the depths forced me to speak to my soul, to call upon her as a living and self-existing being. I had to become aware that I had lost my soul. From this we learn how the spirit of the depths considers the soul: he sees her as a living and self-existing being, and with this he contradicts the spirit of this time for whom the soul is a thing dependent on man, which lets herself be judged and arranged, and whose circumference we can grasp. I had to accept that what I had previously called my soul was not at all my soul, but a dead system. Hence I had to speak to my soul as to something far off and unknown, which did not exist through me, but through whom I existed.[7]

He says: "I had to recognize that I am only the expression and symbol of the soul. In the sense of the spirit of the depths, I am as I am in this visible world a symbol of my soul."[8]

The Feeling-toned Complex: Sensations, Images and Affects

In "The Transcendent Function", Jung recommends taking the affective condition as the point of departure. He suggests that one clarifies the emotion that one sinks into without biases, taking care to objectify through any expressive tools what emerges from this state of concentration. In that manner, the consciousness provides its expressive instruments to the contents of the unconscious and the intrapsychic dialogue can begin. The central role of the affect is fundamental to active imagination. For Jung, affect is synonymous with emotion and its roots in the body. In distinguishing sentiment from affect, Jung emphasizes that well-defined boundaries don't exist, emotion is different from sentiment only with a different degree of intensity. Emotions present bodily innervations which therefore cannot be easily reachable simply through willpower.

Joan Chodorow has greatly illustrated how the affects "function as the bridge between body and psyche".[9]

> An emotion, by definition, is at once somatic and psychic. The somatic aspect is made up of bodily innervations and expressive physical action. The psychic aspect is made up of images and ideas. In psychopathology, the two realms tend to split. By contrast, a naturally felt emotion involves a dialectical relationship – a union of body and psyche.[10]

As we know, the union of body and psyche is implicit in the concept of complex. With regard to the theory of the feeling-toned complexes and to the theory of psychic contagion, Jungian theoretic formulations have been amply validated in the field of neuroscience where a connection between imagination, motor system and emotions can be shown on both an intrapsychic and interpersonal level. With the discovery of mirror neurons, neuroscience has established that the motor system is shaped by an amalgam of interconnected areas with the designated areas of other senses. Initially considered a simple executor, the motor apparatus has become the origin of every sensory, emotional and cognitive information in an interconnected system. These scientific studies have confirmed what humanity has always experienced: there is a connection between the imagination and the proprioceptive system, whether conscious or unconscious. Many Eastern and Western bodily disciplines understand these interactions and know all too well that imagining a movement involves an imperceptible action in musculature. According to the latest research, when one visualizes a scene, areas in the brain are activated as if they were really watching that scene. To imagine a movement involves a modification of certain physiological parameters as if one were actually moving. Furthermore the observation of other people's movements creates a neuronal analog activation. Due to mirror neurons, our brain can relate to the observed movements as our own and therefore it can comprehend the significance of the movements in an immediate way without using any form of reasoning. It's the motor apparatus that understands in an automatic, unconscious and pre-reflexive way. This primary and original bodily understanding seems to correspond to knowing that one knows without knowing how one knows, described by Ester Harding. It refers to how one can have a conscious aware experience as one lets one's body move during the practice of active imagination. Today we know that the emotions as well as movements are understood, reflected and shared by the neuronal system. In fact, it seems that simple observation or being in the presence of other people's emotions stimulates the same neural circuits. Isn't this perhaps an elaboration of the concept of psychic contagion that Jung had already attributed to the sympathetic system and to the corporeal innervations of emotions?

In synthesis, research has demonstrated that a connection between imagination, motor system and emotions exists at a neurophysiological level, just as an unconscious transmission of sensory information exists between us and others. How not to forget the close unity of the sensory, emotional and ideational aspects in Jung's theory of complexes? How not to observe how the general paradigm shift has impacted what scientific researchers observe? How not to re-evaluate not only the role of the body and movement but also the fundamental importance of being in relation to and interdependence with all phenomena? Jung's complex theory, insofar as it expresses the unitary body/psyche system, and the inseparable union of image, emotion and sensation, is not only of great present-day applicability but is likewise of fundamental importance for the practice of active imagination. Complexes seem to display a cyclical, absolute and repetitive memory and tend to remain unchanged as long as they remain in the unconscious. They can however be modified when they begin to appear in consciousness. Bearing in mind Jung's affirmations about the fact that "complexes can have us",[11] it seems important to underscore the need to understand the complexes and to relate to them in a dynamic and flexible way. When we find that we are experiencing a strong emotion, not by choice, but because it happens to us, we always find a need to confront ourselves with the autonomous, automatic, compulsory and repetitive character of the complex which is constellated at that moment. At that point, to avoid the state of possession from the part of the complex extending, it becomes important to identify the voice of the complex, to listen to what the emotional core is telling us, to distinguish oneself from it and to try to relate to it. That can be accomplished using various expressive forms.

In active imagination, the initial state of psychic emptiness, an emptiness "full" of potential, is gradually populated with personifications of the unconscious. Due to the concentration of conscious attitude, these personifications become "pregnant" and modify themselves in the nature of being observed. Unlike the many other imaginative techniques, active imagination emphasizes that the ego doesn't put itself in the shoes of a character as if it were in a psychodrama. Rather, the ego relates with an Other. The ego addresses an image of the unconscious and waits for its response, which can't be foreseen and generally rouses a sensation of surprise.

The personifications of the unconscious speak in an autonomous way and it's important that the ego takes what originates from the unconscious seriously with the same attention and interest that it would if it were talking with someone in real life. After all, Jung didn't ever make clear distinctions between real and unreal: "But the real is what works."[12] Above all, Jung differentiates active imagination from passive fantasies and active imagination from daydreaming. In the first case, and namely in passive fantasies, the ego doesn't have a role. The fantasies are passive as they emerge spontaneously in the conscience without being evoked and thus one observes them without participating. In these cases, there exists the risk of identifying oneself with images that pair up or, on the contrary, images aren't taken seriously and slip away without producing any change in the conscious point of view. In the second case, and namely in the daydreaming, the ego works to its liking with images without relating to them and with their autonomy. By daydreaming, one creates a virtual reality as a defense mechanism that helps one escape from an unsustainable reality and doesn't establish any relationship with the unconscious. One manipulates one's imagination to one's liking and thus the symbolic function cannot work. The imagination is instead active when a real comparison is sought with the other part. The word "active" refers precisely to the fact that the ego, considering the contents of the conscious as real, voluntarily relates to the images that emerge.

Psychic Reality and Symbolic Experience

Active imagination is based on the assumption that the unconscious is real and has subjectivity: "everything goes on functioning in the unconscious state just as though it were conscious. There is perception, thinking, feeling, willpower, and intention, just as though a subject were present".[13] Jung was able to give credibility and respect to his visions and suffered experiences, without being overwhelmed by them and without ceding to the disdainful temptations that his intellect and the spirit of the time generated. Reading *The Red Book*, we learn that the same images that emerged from Jung's unconscious defined themselves as real and required consideration and equal dignity. After all, it was Elia who first laid claim to the gravitas of autonomous existence! It was Elia who taught Jung about the existence of objectivity and about psychic autonomy, and who told him: "We are real and not symbols." And then he added:

> You may call us symbols for the same reason that you can also call your fellow men symbols, if you wish to. But we are just as real as your fellow men. You invalidate nothing and solve nothing by calling us symbols.[14]

Jung responded: "You plunge me into a terrible confusion. Do you wish to be real?" And Elia: "We are certainly what you call real. Here we are, and you have to accept us. The choice is yours."[15]

The essence of active imagination and the attitude that one should take when in conversation with one's own autonomous complexes is explicit and synthesized in a quote in Jung's *Red Book* (it's possible to substitute the devil with any other personification of the unconscious that gives a different point of view with respect to a conscious one):

> I earnestly confronted my devil and behaved with him as with a real person. This I learned in the Mysterium: to take seriously every unknown wanderer who personally inhabits the inner world, since they are real because they are

effectual. It does not help that we say in the spirit of this time: there is no devil. There was one with me. This took place in me. I did with him what I could. I could speak with him. . . . I must have it out with him, as I cannot expect that he as an independent personality would accept my standpoint without further ado. I would be fleeing if I did not try to come to an understanding with him. If ever you have the rare opportunity to speak with the devil, then do not forget to confront him in all seriousness. He is your devil after all. The devil as the adversary is your own other standpoint; he tempts you and sets a stone in your path where you least want it. Taking the devil seriously does not mean going over to his side, or else one becomes the devil. Rather it means coming to an understanding. Thereby you accept your other standpoint. With that the devil fundamentally loses ground, and so do you. And that may be well and good. . . . In such a manner, I arrive at his seriousness, and with this we reach common ground where understanding is possible.[16]

Active Imagination in Movement

Jung has always considered body and psyche two aspects of the same thing, but little space has been given to the body as a central clinical tool in Jungian training. We are now living a paradigm shift towards the importance of the right brain in the psychotherapeutic process as well as towards the recognition of the value of emotions and images as bridges between body and psyche. The Jungian clinical approach to bodily experience needs to be further developed. There is a strong call for updated training which may include a growing awareness of bodily felt sensations, somatic images, non-verbal communications in the therapeutic relationship. Analysis cannot ignore the weight of somatic unconscious, body communications, somatic countertransference. Every cell of the body is equipped with intelligence and memory. The most recent scientific theories confirm not only the close inter-relationship of diverse body systems, but also the localization of the mind in the entire body and not solely in the brain. The memory of traumatic experiences remains in the body and thus activating the symbolic capacity of the body can help reconnect one to those memories in order to overcome them and recreate a bridge between the event and the memory.

In his writings on active imagination, Jung suggests there are many ways to experience, express, communicate and transform the unconscious (predominantly affects by way of images) through any number of forms, including dance and movement-based active imagination, often followed by writing and other forms of expression. The conscious–unconscious relationship can be explored across spontaneous and self-directed expression of the body in movement. The practice of active imagination through movement is notably appreciated and valued in the international sphere. For many years, the IAAP (International Association of Analytical Psychology) Congresses have dedicated a pre-congress day to theoretical, clinical and experiential exploration of this method. "By listening to the body to access and express the imagination, individuals may discover inner-directed movement as a way to bridge the realms of conscious and unconscious, body and psyche, instinct and spirit, affect and image, memory and emergence" (online description of IAAP pre-congress workshop). It's an honor for me to be part of this international group that promotes research about a practice that's extremely innovative and rich with possibility. The international group, coordinated by Joan Chodorow, collects the contributions of participating colleagues from many different countries. In the proceedings of the IAAP Congresses, some of these contributions are available to read.[17]

Dance/movement as active imagination makes it possible to perceive psyche and body as a unity within which a series of bridges allow for passage and communication between one and the other. Bridges are vital elements for psychophysical health because they allow communication while maintaining distinct differences. In a state of heightened awareness, the vital tension between the opposites allows the emergence of new possibilities. As known in Jungian psychology, it's very important to maintain a thriving relationship between opposites while not being oppressed or crucified by them when extreme conflicts occur. In this way, we should be able to flow from one position to another and allow transcendent function to activate, so that a different psychic situation can emerge. Having opposite elements together with no confusion means to be able to activate the symbolic capacity of the consciousness and to overcome the symptom: the symbol that holds the known and the not yet known together is the third element that can transform the psychic energy and can allow an agreement between antagonistic elements. The emergence of the third element contains both poles but at the same time transcends them, creating a new synthesis and therefore new opportunities.

How does the experience occur? One closes one's eyes and listens to one's own sensations while letting the unconscious come up through spontaneous body movements. At the outset of an experience of active imagination with the body, the dialectical tension between the ego and the unconscious is expressed in the relationship between conscious movement and letting oneself be moved by the unknown. Gradually, one is able to shape the contents of the unconscious in a continuous interaction of the sensory, emotive and imaginary realm. This method, like many others, requires a long and patient training. If the ego is truly open and attentive, the unconscious images will be able to embody themselves in the forms which will make them most easily recognizable. Often the ego is surprised to find itself within one of these bodily forms, and it can then choose to actively explore these forms by using the qualities of movement corresponding to the moment at hand.[18] The form of the body can condition or stimulate the emergence, in the here and now, of specific images from the unconscious, just like specific unconscious images activated by the conscience can cause the bodily form to modify. The forms of the body and the psychic images model themselves on one another. Usually one activates a circular and recursive process whereby every aspect is simultaneously produced. It isn't easy to explain in words a situation this complex. Through the experience of moving and being moved the physical body is shaped by images of the psyche that in its turn gives them form. The ego surrenders to Self-direct movement while maintaining an alert, active point of view. Dance, by its very nature, tends to create links between what is inside and what is outside.

> The kinesthetic sense, that belongs to muscular perception, is the only sense that lets us perceive the internal world and the external world, since it is activated by proprioceptors that are sensitive to both internal and external stimuli; therefore, the kinesthetic sense acts as a bridge between the unconscious and consciousness, or between the inside and the outside.[19]

When the body is moved to promote the confrontation between consciousness and the unconscious, it is no longer possible to maintain the separation Western consciousness has always imposed between the outside world we observe and the internal world we perceive. They go together. In the paradox of dance, the union of psyche and matter seems to take shape. In the experience of moving and letting oneself be moved, images that want to be embodied sometimes emerge from the unconscious; in these cases, "the experience shifts from dancing with a particular image to allowing oneself to be danced by it".[20]

> Thus, it is the matter of the physical body that is moulded by the images of the psyche and which, in turn, gives them form. Giving form to the images does not mean identifying with them. It means having at one's disposal that intrapsychic distance that permits the ego and the imagination to be present together, each with its own autonomy, in the same body, without compromising our consciousness nor our contact with the unconscious. Only acceptance of the paradox can make such an event comprehensible.[21]

The vibrations become audible, the images are visible, the perceptions are palpable, the emotions are tangible. The dance becomes the visible manifestation of interior sound. Psyche and matter, body and soul are actually perceived as a unity and the incarnated imagination carries out its function as a bridge between the two. The body becomes the instrument and vessel of experience which produces a paradoxical situation. Paradox seems to be the first and last reality of matter, as quantum physics has emphasized and as Jung always pointed out. Paradox is revealed in the very nature of the unconscious, as it appears to us in dreams; it is innate in the Universe, in which order and disorder coexist, "it is by disintegrating that the cosmos organizes itself".[22] Paradox is the language of the Oriental mystic traditions, like Taoism. "The spirit of the depths took my understanding and all my knowledge and placed them at the service of the inexplicable and the paradoxical".[23]

In our attempts to investigate psychic or material reality, everything which cannot be grasped with a logical and rational attitude can be expressed by paradoxes. It is perhaps the only language that makes it possible to express the vital tension between the opposites which touch one another but do not merge, the polarities that can be present simultaneously, without one losing itself in the other. In the alchemical procedure that Jung used as a metaphor, both for the analytical relationship and active imagination, the union of opposites could come about in a third, new element, "a transcendental entity that could be described only in paradoxes".[24] The union of opposites can be achieved by surrendering oneself to the paradoxical essence of reality, and giving shape to images and emotions through the expression of the body. The ego enters actively into the choreographic dialogue that translates the dialectic tension between surrender and will, as M.S. Whitehouse has described for us:

> I want to describe the paradox in which the opposites are united: each becomes the other. This is the ideal – it is what is meant by both/and instead of either/or. There is a saying that comes from Tao. It was not intended primarily for movement but it gives the whole of movement awareness a framework. "Non-action in action; action in non-action". Both pairs are in each half of the total saying. They cannot be opposed; they go together.[25]

Thus, consciousness and the unconscious, each with equal dignity, can become true partners in dialogue.

Authentic Movement in the Consulting Room

Dance/Movement as a form of Active Imagination (also called Authentic Movement) is defined by a mover (analysand), a witness (analyst) and the dynamics of their relationship. The mover moves with eyes closed in the presence of a witness, whose task it is to hold and contain the experience of the person moving. The mover–witness relationship offers a container to explore in a safe way inner emotions, body awareness, ancient memories stored in our cells, multi-sensory images, future possibilities. Active imagination in movement provides an opportunity to share and explore bridges between intrapsychic dynamics and interpersonal relationship to further develop a symbolic perspective, towards developing ongoing awareness of the body/psyche connection as a central clinical tool.

> When we use our bodies to express the imagination, the vividness of the sensory-motor experience tends to take us to complexes that were constellated in infancy or early childhood. . . . Just as the imagination takes us to the emotional core of a complex, it can also leads us *through* it. . . . This means developing the ability to bear the emotion that is stirred when a complex is touched, and at the same time imagine and explore symbolically the images that are part of it.[26]

They can activate very archaic channels of expression; ancient memories linked to psychic complexes can emerge, invested in strong emotional charge. A situation of that kind could be overwhelming if the complex of the ego and its defensive system weren't prepared to face that dialogue. It's fundamental that there's a sufficiently solid, flexible and differentiated Ego. The protected space of the consulting room is the ideal place to be able to face a journey this delicate. Active imagination in movement requires the presence of the analyst. When we move, we are only inside, we cannot see our own dance from the outside, or observe from the outside the object we have created. The process of creation is the creation itself that disappears when the work is finished. When the dance is over, it no longer exists, except in the memory and the atmosphere of the one who has seen it and the one who has danced it. This is one of the reasons why the need for a witness, an external observer, arose as active imagination began to be practiced through bodily expression. Certainly, today it's possible to film and record the experience so that it can be seen again but the presence of the analyst involves a much deeper role.

The experience is then transcribed or verbalized to the analyst, who acts as a witness. Often it's precisely in the moment in which one writes or in which one directs oneself to the Other outside, recounting what has just happened (in an analog way as one does with dreams) that something clarifies itself or an intuition arrives at the consciousness. The verbalization is an integral/essential part of the process that doesn't get interpreted or judged. The analysed/mover can give a shape to the dynamic tension between consciousness and the unconscious, can let every part of himself/herself emerge, knowing that it will be accepted by the analyst/witness without any judgement or interpretation. And at the moment of verbal dialogue the mover will be able to recognize himself/herself in the presence of the Other. This enhances our ability to trust and to establish relationships. Trusting a witness leads us to have renewed trust in ourselves and in the creative resources lying within each of us. The analyst's eye contact allows the analyzed to sink into the experience. The observing eye provides the torch to descend into the darkness of the unexplored abysses of the "body-psyche"; it also helps to contain fears. This eye is the symbol of consciousness and fertility; it reflects the movers and the movers reflect themselves in it; it is the eye of the Other, the eye that recognizes, helps to relate to and to integrate the experience in a conscious process of transformation. Usually healing or other simpler transformations coincide with an expansion of awareness, which thus promote an expansion of boundaries and enable the possibility to understand things from multiple points of view. Active imagination is one of the methods that relates to its own unconscious and fosters the process of individuation. Every individuation process asks that unknown parts of one's total personality can gradually emerge, in other words, be seen, recognized and integrated as one's own. The capacity to be in relationship with the other, both from within and outside ourselves, is fundamental to the individuation process. When one has a relationship with one's own unconscious, one can see things more clearly; when one is possessed by one's own emotions and projections, one has a distorted vision of reality.

Even though Jung repeatedly emphasized that active imagination was to be accomplished in solitude and unmediated by the analyst's presence in order to allow a direct contact with one's own unconscious, he nevertheless welcomed the possibility that in certain cases active imagination could be done directly in the presence of the analyst. This can be witnessed from his experience and from the publications of Joan Chodorow, Anita Green, Tina Keller, Margarita Mendez, Renate Oppikofer, Tina Stromsted, and many others.[27] In the introduction to a volume that gathers the writings of Jung about active imagination, Joan Chodorow (1997) demonstrates the different aspects of Jungian thought, his richness of thinking and multifaceted approach and the way the role of the analyst is interrogated with respect to active imagination. Jung always sustained that active imagination can facilitate the separation of the patient from the analyst in so far as it promotes an independence anchored by one's own individuation process. Underscoring this aspect, Joan Chodorow draws attention to how, in some cases, active imagination can also be an intrinsic element of the analysis and reiterates that Jung recommended the analyst not to intervene. When the unconscious image had taken form, Jung encouraged patients to relate to it and he preferred to not interpret images of active imagination. The role of the analyst is also that of mediating the transcendent function, maintaining an open channel between the conscious and unconscious. In that way, Jung recognized that the analyst cannot cure without engaging their own conscious and unconscious reactions. "This inner-directed way of working has enormous power. When the analyst is able to hold the opposites within, the patient is free to do the same."[28] With this viewpoint, active imagination involves an analytic relationship:

> For some, intrapsychic conflict can be contained and expressed symbolically through a series of internal dialogues and other forms of active imagination. For others, the tension between conscious and unconscious will arrive best to the conscience through external dialogues, interactions with others. . . . For some, freedom requires learning to be oneself in the presence of another. For others, it's essential to work alone. Everyone is unique. In my opinion, Jung didn't believe in dogmatic rules and presented his ideas leaving a lot of space for variation and for creative possibilities.[29]

In order to begin active imagination, it's fundamental to confront and overcome fear, to prepare for the descent and the comeback. Although Jung, in *The Red Book*, emphasizes the need for solitude as a necessary path along a journey, he also admonishes the need for not being alone:

> It is wisdom to fear oneself. Only the heroes say that they are fearless. But you know what happens to the hero. With fear and trembling, looking around yourselves with mistrust, go thus into the depths, but do not do this alone; two or more is greater security since the depths are full of murder. Also secure yourselves the way of retreat. Go cautiously, . . . The depths are stronger than us; so do not be heroes, be clever and drop the heroics, since nothing is more dangerous than to play the hero. The depths want to keep you.[30]

The rituals of the therapeutic setting evoke energetic fields in which invisible, unexpressed contents can gradually find a space to be reflected. Working in the healing sphere, the analyst prepares, gathers, contains and restores through the use of eye contact and silence. When active imagination is practiced in the analytical setting, the ritual form becomes even more powerful, and allows entry to the energy field of the therapeutic relationship. In a heightened state of conscience and in the guarantee of containment, the mover can confront the unknown. The ritual form passes through the threshold of the complexual possession in order to open up to the generating force of new connections and to be confronted with the mysterious and transcendent dimension of life. "The individuated ego feels object to an unknown and superior subject."[31] Body engagement can bring us not only towards ancient memories but also towards our future, liberating new energies.

The starting point of active imagination can be a state of emptiness, where the wanderer is in the dark, moving towards unexplored spaces where neither crossed paths nor guiding lights exist, and where there aren't maps for orientation. It's a journey through the darkness of the sea in order to discover new lands, where the light of the conscience seeks to encounter the hidden light of the unconscious. Active imagination, as a method of self-healing, can also be a true initiatory journey. One must depart empty-handed, leaving behind everything in order to enter emptiness "full" of potential. This in turn allows for deep and radical transformations. A true journey also means the willingness to deal with that side of ourselves that wants to leave everything just as it is. Therefore one has to bring the torch of one's own awareness. This is part of the great process of individuation, a process which entails the ability to stay related to the unconscious even as we emerge out of its undifferentiated aspects. Transformation comes about through an endless series of deaths and rebirths in an analog way like ancient celebrations of the Mysteries. In the thick of the woods we risk stumbling along in total darkness with not so much as a compass or a torch, or going round in circles among the prickly thorns, without meeting anyone who might point out the path. We might catch a glimpse of a light, run after it, only to see it go out and lose all sense of bearing once again. But all at once, the path might just appear, right under our feet, to make us realize that the right way is the one we were already on. Active imagination in movement connects one to the Greek origin of the term "myo", to keep the mouth and the eyes closed in the search of silence. It's above all closing the eyes and welcoming silence in a protected space that allows the interior view to open and one's sense of proprioception to intensify. It's a powerful and efficient method that helps recover that integrated intuitive-sensory-imaginative-emotional-cognitive-spiritual knowledge with an ancient knowledge usually lost. By means of active imagination, one travels to unknown territories, sometimes terrifying, and what characterizes the veracity of experience is the surprise of the ego before the unforeseen responses from that which is absolutely "other". The mystery, the astonishment before the "foreign foreigner",[32] causes the emergence of a new direction. Psychic balance calls for the creation of symbols capable of holding opposites together, and enable us to be open to new prospects. Practicing active imagination in movement is to dive into an unseen and unknown world; it can be described as a process of transformation within a mystical experience where it is possible to perceive ourselves as symbols of the soul.

Authentic Movement as a Collective Practice

Authentic Movement is a dynamic form, in continual evolution; its pluralistic and differentiated nature reveals its extreme adaptability and its potential transforming effectiveness in different areas of life. Authentic Movement offers us the opportunity to promote a confrontation, not only between the polarities innate in our psyche, but also between what is within us and what is outside of us. When practiced in a group, in its continuous alternation of roles between mover and witness, Authentic Movement offers us an external echo of what happens between the poles within the psyche. It reflects and activates the fluctuations in the individual and collective psyche and allows us to enter into the very rhythm of life, gradually increasing our awareness. Thus the crystallization of positions is hindered. The discipline of Authentic Movement grounds the arrival of spiritual experiences and creates the field for the emergence of archetypal images and synchronistic events.

Authentic Movement as a collective practice creates a sacred space inside the circle of witnesses and promotes mystical experiences.

This is what happens when the right thing occurs at the right time. Everyone has his eyes closed and moves spontaneously, listening to his own Self, yet it seems as if everyone were being directed from above (or from below?), that precise directions were being given so that every movement is adapted to the other. Each body moves as if it were being guided by an external choreographer that arranges all the elements. Or perhaps there is a choreographer within each individual body? Or is it simply that the body knows and sees? All the parts prove to be dependent upon one another, the movements seem to call to one another and the collective body moves in its differentiated unity. Suddenly, from the initial chaos everything seems to fall into place, everything seems to follow an inscrutable order. The system organizes itself. Sometimes it seems as if there were an underground communication on the unconscious level. Sometimes there are significant coincidences between what each person is living in his or her own individual psyche and what is happening outside, among the other individuals, in the circle as a whole. There is an identity of meaning between internal and external reality, between the individual body and the collective body. The meeting between conscious and unconscious, between internal and external, between psyche and matter, seems to activate Jung's principle of synchronicity. . . . It seems that psyche and matter are manifested in their basic unity: the *Unus Mundus*.[33]

Within the complex experience of Authentic Movement we have a chance to experience the *Unus Mundus*, to feel the *Anima Mundi*, to live the interconnectedness of unconscious events while perceiving interdependence and the sense of the manifold unity of the world. Authentic Movement offers an opportunity for participants to share and explore bridges between intrapsychic dynamics and interpersonal relationship to further develop a symbolic perspective, towards developing ongoing awareness of the body/psyche connection as a central clinical tool. It promotes healing and creative process through individual and collective transformative journeys. Authentic Movement offers plurality of perspectives and allow us to open ourselves to those new visions of the world that are characterized by tolerance, cooperation, solidarity in the face of uncertainty, conflict and competition.

I'd like to conclude with an image that Jung offers us from *The Red Book*: the image of the Chariot and the Charioteer. Referring to the metaphor of the chariot and the charioteer, Jung tells us that at times intention and determination pit us against our destiny. If our intention and determination are too strong, and aren't in harmony with the wish of the Self, with the invisible order or with the common good, these will strongly contrast with non-power and nonsense. Thus Jung says that wisdom is knowing how to be the Charioteer of an invisible Chariot that leads us. With an open attitude towards mystery and towards the spiritual dimension of life, we will be greatly capable of welcoming the incomprehensible. Jung enables us to learn that if we welcome the symbol and we nourish it like a newborn, the symbol itself will be our Charioteer and we will experience ourselves as symbols of the soul.

Notes

1 Jung, [1916]1957/1958, pp. 89–90.
2 Jung, 2012, p.122.
3 Jung, 2012, p.139.
4 Jung, 2012, p.162.
5 Jung, 2012, p.133.
6 Jung, 2012, p.384.
7 Jung, 2012, p.139.
8 Ibid., p. 134.
9 Chodorow, 1991, p. 41.
10 Jung, 1934, p. 96.
11 Chodorow, 1991, p. 3.
12 Jung, 1928, p. 217.
13 Jung, 1947–1954, p. 186.
14 Jung, 2012, p. 187.
15 Ibid., p. 187.
16 Jung, 2012, p. 218.
17 IAAP Congress Proceedings 2005, 2009, 2012, 2014, 2017, 2020.
18 Adorisio, 1995, 2005, 2007, 2013, 2019; Chodorow, 1978, 1984, 1991, 1992, 1995, 1997.
19 Adorisio, 2007, pp. 85–86.
20 Chodorow, 1991, p. 126.
21 Adorisio, 2007, p. 86.
22 Morin, 1994, p. 57.
23 Jung, 2012, p. 120.

24 Jung, 1955/56, p. 536.
25 Whitehouse, 1979, p. 83.
26 Chodorow, 1991, p. 6.
27 IAAP Congress Proceedings 2005, 2009, 2012, 2014, 2017, 2020; Chodorow, 1997, 2006; Keller, 2011.
28 Chodorow, 1997, pp. 14–15.
29 Chodorow, 1997, p. 17.
30 Jung, 2012, p. 168.
31 Jung 1928, p. 240.
32 Otto, 1966, p. 35.
33 Adorisio, 2007, p. 90.

References

Adorisio, A. (1995). "Il corpo e l'immaginazione attiva", in *Rivista di Psicologia Analitica* n. 51. Rome: Astrolabio, pp. 161–180.

Adorisio, A. (2005). "Bellezza Orsini and creativity: Images of body and soul from a sixteenth-century prison", *Spring Journal*, n. 72: "Body and Soul". New Orleans, Lousiana: Spring Journal Books, pp. 281–297.

Adorisio, A. (2007). "Moving toward complexity: The myth of Echo and Narcissus", in Pallaro, P. (ed.), *Authentic Movement: Moving the Body, Moving the Self, Being Moved*, vol. 2. London and Philadelphia: Jessica Kingsley Publishers, pp. 80–96.

Adorisio A. (2013). "L'immaginazione attiva. Origini ed evoluzione", in *Quaderni di Cultura Junghiana – Rivista online del CIPA – Istituto di Roma*, pp. 60–72.

Adorisio A. (2019). "Il movimento Autentico come mandala del cuore in Atti Convegno ANEB, Milano 2019". *Il corpo come mandala dell'universo*, pp. 218–232, Milan: Aneb 2020.

Chodorow, J. (1984). "To move and to be moved", in Pallaro, P. (ed.) (1999), *Authentic Movement: Essays by Mary Starks Whitehouse, Janet Adler and Chodorow* (pp. 267–278). London: Jessica Kingsley Publishers.

Chodorow, J. (1991). *Dance Therapy & Depth Psychology – The Moving Imagination.* London: Routledge.

Chodorow, J. (1995). "The body as symbol: Dance/movement in analysis", in Pallaro, P. (ed.) (1999), *Authentic Movement: Essays by Mary Starks Whitehouse, Janet Adler and Chodorow* (pp. 279–300). London: Jessica Kingsley Publishers.

Chodorow, J. (1997). *C.G. Jung on Active Imagination.* New York & London: Routledge.

Chodorow J. (2006). "Active Imagination", in Papadopoulos. R.K. (ed.), *The Handbook of Jungian Psychology.* New York: Routledge (pp. 215–243).

Harding, M.E. (1971). *Woman's Mysteries – Ancient and Modern.* (1990). Boston & Shaftesbury: Shambala.

IAAP Congress Proceedings

2005. Adorisio, A., Chodorow, J., Grant Fay, C., Green, A., Gerson, J., Mendez, M., Oppikofer, R., Stromsted, T. & Wyman-McGinty, W. "Edges of the embodied experience: The moving imagination, pre-congress day", in *Edges of Experience: Memory and Emergence – IAAP Congress Proceedings, Barcelona 2004*. Edited by L. Cowan. Einsiedeln: Daimon Verlag AG.

2009. Adorisio, A., Chodorow, J., Grant Fay, C., Green, A., Gerson, J., Mendez, M. & Stromsted, T. "Moving Journeys – embodied encounters: The living body in analysis, pre-congress day", in *Journeys, Encounters: Clinical, Communal, Cultural – IAAP Congress Proceedings*, Cape Town 2007. Edited by P. Bennett, Einsiedeln: Daimon Verlag AG.

2012. Adorisio, A., Chodorow, J., Green, A., Gerson, J., Mendez, M., Oppikofer, R. & Stromsted, T. "Pre-congress workshop on movement as active imagination – Multiplicity in the living, moving body: psyche, nature, culture", in *Facing Multiplicity: Psyche, Nature, Culture – IAAP Congress Proceedings – Montreal 2010*. Edited by P. Bennett, Einsiedeln: Daimon Verlag AG.

2014. Adorisio, A., Chodorow, J., Green, A., Gerson, J., Mendez, M., Oppikofer, R. & Stromsted, T. "Copenhagen 2013–100 years on: Origins, innovations and controversies", in *Proceedings of the 19th Congress of the International Association for Analytical Psychology-Copenhagen 2013*. Edited by Emilija Kiehl, Einsiedeln: Daimon Verlag AG.

2017. Adorisio, A., Chodorow, J., Hirai, T., Mendez, M., Stromsted, T., & Sakiyama, S. "Pre-congress workshop – Authentic movement: Dance & moving active imagination" in *XXth IAAP Congress Proceedings, Kyoto 2016*. Edited by Emilija Kiehl and Margaret Klenck Daimon, Einsiedeln: Daimon Verlag.

2020. Adorisio, A., Chodorow, J., Mendez, M. & Stromsted, T. "Active Imagination in movement", in *XXI IAAP Congress Proceedings, Vienna 2019 – Encountering the Other: Within Us, Between Us and in the World*. Edited by Kiehl E. & Egli J. Einsiedeln: Daimon Verlag.

Jung, C.G. ([1916]1957/1958). "The transcendent function", in *The Collected Works*. vol. 8. (1969/1978). Princeton, NJ: Princeton University Press.

Jung, C.G. (1928). "The relations between the ego and the unconscious", in *The Collected Works*. vol. 7. (1970). London: Routledge & Kegan Paul.

Jung, C.G.(1934). "A review of the complex theory", in *The Collected Works*, vol. 8. (1975). Princeton, NJ: Princeton University Press.

Jung, C.G. (1935). "The Tavistock Lectures. On the theory and practice of analytical psychology", in *The Collected Works*, vol. 18 (1977). London: Routledge & Kegan Paul.

Jung, C.G. (1936a). "The concept of the collective unconscious", in *The Collected Works*, vol. 9.I (1968). Princeton, NJ: Princeton University Press.

Jung, C.G. (1947–1954). "On the nature of the Psyche", in *The Collected Works*, vol. 8 (1972), London: Routledge & Kegan Paul.

Jung, C.G. (1955/56). "Mysterium Coniunctionis", in *The Collected Works*, vol. 14 (1974). Princeton, NJ: Princeton University Press.

Jung, C.G. (1951). "Appendix: on syncronicity", in *The Collected Works*, vol. 8 (1969). Princeton NJ: Princeton University Press.

Jung, C.G. (1952–1969). "Synchronicity: An acasual connecting principle", in *The Collected Works*, vol. 8. Princeton NJ: Princeton University Press.

Jung, C.G. (1961). *Memories, Dreams, Reflections* (1989). New York: Vintage Books Edition.

Jung, C.G. (2012). *The Red Book – Liber Novus*, S. Shamdasani, (Ed.), Philemon Series, New York: The Philemon Foundation & W.W. Norton & Company (or. Ed. 2009).

Keller, T. (2011). *The Memoir of Tina-Keller Jenny: A Lifelong Confrontation with the Psychology of C.G. Jung*, edited by W.K. Swan. New Orleans: Spring Journal Books.

Morin, E. (1994). *Il Metodo. Ordine disordine e organizzazione*. Milan: Feltrinelli. Original French edition 1977.

Otto, R. (1966). *Il sacro* (1994). Milan: Feltrinelli.

Pallaro, P. (ed.) (1999). *Authentic Movement: Essays by Mary Starks Whitehouse, Janet Adler and Chodorow*. London: Jessica Kingsley Publishers.

Pallaro, P. (ed.) (2007). *Authentic Movement: Moving the Body, Moving the Self, Being Moved*, vol. 2. London and Philadelphia: Jessica Kingsley Publishers.

Shamdasani, S. (2009). "Introduction to the *Red Book* of C.G. Jung", in Jung, C.G. (2012), *The Red Book – Liber Novus*, Shamdasani, S. (ed.). New York: Philemon Series, The Philemon Foundation & W.W. Norton & Company.

Von Franz, M.L. (1978). "L'immaginazione attiva", in *Rivista di psicologia Analitica*, n. 17, Rome: Astrolabio, pp. 75–87.

Whitehouse, M.S. (1979). "C.G. Jung and dance-therapy: Two major principles", in Pallaro, P. (ed.) (1999), *Authentic Movement: Essays by Mary Starks Whitehouse, Janet Adler and Joan Chodorow*. London: Jessica Kingsley Publishers.

Index

Please note that page references to Figures will be in **bold**, while references to Tables are in *italics*. Footnotes will be denoted by the letter 'n' and Note number following the page number.

For Product Safety Concerns and Information please contact our EU
representative GPSR@taylorandfrancis.com
Taylor & Francis Verlag GmbH, Kaufingerstraße 24, 80331 München, Germany

*9 7 8 1 0 3 2 5 3 3 0 0 1 *